CONTENTS

A NOTE ABOUT COPYRIGHT

AAT

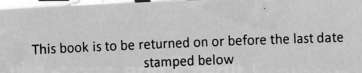

Q...stions and answers ... (QCF)
A... D1...

'LE...EL 2 CERTIFICATE IN ACCOUNTING
(Q...

QUESTION BANK

...actions

Edition

For as...

Second edition June 2014
ISBN 9781 4727 0931 8

Previous edition
ISBN 9781 4727 0347 7

British Library Cataloguing-in-Publication Data
A catalogue record for this book is available from the British Library

Published by
BPP Learning Media Ltd
BPP House
Aldine Place
London W12 8AA

www.bpp.com/learningmedia

Printed in the United Kingdom by Martins of Berwick
Sea View Works
Spittal
Berwick-Upon-Tweed
TD15 1RS

BPP
LEARNING MEDIA

INTRODUCTION

This is BPP Learning Media's AAT Question Bank for Processing Bookkeeping Transactions. It is part of a suite of ground breaking resources produced by BPP Learning Media for the AAT's assessments under the Qualification and Credit Framework.

Processing Bookkeeping Transactions is **computer assessed**. As well as being available in the traditional paper format, this **Question Bank is available in an online environment** containing tasks similar to those you will encounter in the AAT's testing environment. BPP Learning Media believe that the best way to practise for an online assessment is in an online environment. However, if you are unable to practise in the online environment you will find that all tasks in the paper Question Bank have been written in a style that is as close as possible to the style that you will be presented with in your online assessment.

This Question Bank has been written in conjunction with the BPP Text, and has been carefully designed to enable students to practise all of the learning outcomes and assessment criteria for Processing Bookkeeping Transactions. It is fully up to date as at June 2014 and reflects both the AAT's unit guide and the sample assessment provided by the AAT.

This Question Bank contains these key features:

- Tasks corresponding to each chapter of the Text. Some tasks are designed for learning purposes, others are of assessment standard

- The AAT's AQ2013 sample assessments and answers for Processing Bookkeeping Transactions and further BPP practice assessments

The emphasis in all tasks and assessments is on the practical application of the skills acquired.

VAT

You may find tasks throughout this Question Bank that need you to calculate or be aware of a rate of VAT. This is stated at 20% in these examples and questions.

Approaching the assessment

When you sit the assessment it is very important that you follow the on screen instructions. This means you need to carefully read the instructions, both on the introduction screens and during specific tasks.

When you access the assessment you should be presented with an introductory screen with information similar to that shown below (taken from the introductory screen from one of the AAT's sample assessments for Processing Bookkeeping Transactions).

We have provided the following assessment to help you familiarise yourself with AAT's e-assessment environment. It is designed to demonstrate as many as possible of the question types you may find in a live assessment. It is not designed to be used on its own to determine whether you are ready for a live assessment.

Each task is independent. You will not need to refer to your answers to previous tasks.
Read every task carefully to make sure you understand what is required.

Where the date is relevant, it is given in the task data.

Both minus signs and brackets can be used to indicate negative numbers UNLESS task instructions say otherwise.

You must use a full stop to indicate a decimal point.
For example, write 100.57 NOT 100,57 or 100 57

You may use a comma to indicate a number in the thousands, but you don't have to.
For example, 10000 and 10,000 are both OK.

Other indicators are not compatible with the computer-marked system.

Complete all 10 tasks.

The tasks in are set in a business situation where the following apply:

- You are employed by the business, Gold, as a bookkeeper.
- Gold uses a manual bookkeeping system.
- Double entry takes place in the general ledger. Individual accounts of trade receivables and trade payables are kept in the sales and purchases ledgers as subsidiary accounts.
- The cash-book and petty cash-book should be treated as part of the double entry system unless the task instructions state otherwise.
- The VAT rate is 20%.

The actual instructions will vary depending on the subject you are studying for. It is very important you read the instructions on the introductory screen and apply them in the assessment. You don't want to lose marks when you know the correct answer just because you have not entered it in the right format.

In general, the rules set out in the AAT sample assessment(s) for the subject you are studying for will apply in the real assessment, but you should again read the information on this screen in the real assessment carefully just to make sure. This screen may also confirm the VAT rate used if applicable.

A full stop is needed to indicate a decimal point. We would recommend using minus signs to indicate negative numbers and leaving out the comma signs to indicate thousands, as this results in a lower number of key strokes and less margin for error when working under time pressure. Having said that, you can use whatever is easiest for you as long as you operate within the rules set out for your particular assessment.

You should therefore complete all of the tasks. Don't leave questions unanswered.

In some assessments written or complex tasks may be human marked. In this case you are given a blank space or table to enter your answer into. You are told in assessments which tasks these are (note: there may be none if all answers are marked by the computer).

If these involve calculations, it is a good idea to decide in advance how you are going to lay out your answers to such tasks by practising answering them on a Word document, and certainly you should try all such tasks in this question bank and in the AAT's environment using the sample/practice assessments.

When asked to fill in tables, or gaps, never leave any blank even if you are unsure of the answer. Fill in your best estimate.

Note that for some assessments where there is a lot of scenario information or tables of data provided (eg tax tables), you may need to access these via 'pop-ups'. Instructions will be provided on how you can bring up the necessary data during the assessment.

Finally, take note of any task specific instructions once you are in the assessment. For example you may be asked to enter a date in a certain format or to enter a number to a certain number of decimal places.

Remember you can practice the BPP questions in this question bank in an online environment on our dedicated AAT Online page. On the same page is a link to the current AAT sample assessments as well.

If you have any comments about this book, please email ianblackmore@bpp.com or write to Ian Blackmore, AAT Range Manager, BPP Learning Media Ltd, BPP House, Aldine Place, London W12 8AA.

Question bank

Processing Bookkeeping Transactions Question bank

All answers should be rounded to the nearest penny unless otherwise instructed.

Chapter 1 Business documentation

Task 1.1

For each of the following transactions state whether they are cash or credit transactions:

	Cash transaction ✓	Credit transaction ✓
Purchase of goods for £200 payable by cash in one week's time		
Writing a cheque for the purchase of a new computer		
Sale of goods to a customer where the invoice accompanies the goods		
Receipt of a cheque from a customer for goods purchased today		
Purchase of goods where payment is due in three weeks' time		

Task 1.2

When a supplier delivers goods to a customer, the customer will expect to receive in due course:

✓	
	A credit note
	A remittance advice
	A petty cash voucher
✓	An invoice

Task 1.3

Ken trades in exotic dress materials. He has a large number of small suppliers. He likes to keep all invoices and credit notes from each supplier together in a file for that supplier.

Which sort of coding system would be most appropriate for Ken to use when devising a unique code number for each supplier?

✓	
	An alpha-numeric system
	A numeric system

Chapter 2 Discounts and VAT

Task 2.1

Ken trades in exotic dress materials. He has many credit customers who operate in the same trade as him and he routinely offers these customers a discount off the list price of his goods in order to maintain good relations. This is an example of:

✓	
✓	A trade discount
	A settlement discount
	A bulk discount
	A discount for prompt payment

Task 2.2

VAT is a tax on consumer expenditure which a VAT registered business must collect from its customers and pay over to

✓	
	The Home Office
	The Treasury
	The Inland Revenue
✓	HM Revenue & Customs

Task 2.3

On your desk is a pile of sales invoices that have already had the price of the goods entered onto them and been totalled.

You now have to calculate and deduct the 15% trade discount that is allowed on each of these invoices.

Goods total	Trade discount £	Net total £
£416.80	62.52	354.28
£105.60	15.8	
£96.40	14.	81.99
£263.20		2
£351.00	52.65	298.35

Task 2.4

There is a further pile of invoices which have the net total entered for which you are required to calculate the VAT charge and the invoice total.

Net total	VAT £	Gross total £
£258.90	51.76	10.68
£316.80	63.36	80.16
£82.60	16.52	99.12
£152.70	30.54	18.24
£451.30	90.26	541.54

Task 2.5

You now discover that for each of the invoices from the previous activity a 3% settlement discount has been offered.

Recalculate the VAT charge to correctly reflect the settlement discount and show the revised gross total (remember that VAT is always rounded down to the nearest penny).

Net total	VAT £	Gross total £
£258.90	51.78	
£316.80		
£82.60		
£152.70		
£451.30		

Task 2.6

The following gross totals include VAT (no settlement discount is available).

Calculate the amount of VAT on each invoice and the net amount of the invoice:

Gross total £	VAT £	Net total £
145.20		
66.90		
246.60		
35.40		
125.40		

Task 2.7

The following purchases have been made for cash inclusive of VAT.

Calculate the amount of VAT on each purchase and the net amount of the purchase:

Gross total £	VAT £	Net total £
252.66		
169.20		
48.60		
104.28		
60.48		
822.60		

Chapter 3 The books of prime entry

Task 3.1

Ken trades in exotic dress materials. He sends an invoice for goods of £100 plus VAT to a customer. No discounts apply. The gross total will be:

£

Task 3.2

Ken sends an invoice for goods of £100 plus VAT to a customer to whom he allows a 10% trade discount. The gross total will be:

£

Task 3.3

Natural Productions is a small business that manufactures a variety of soaps and bath products which it sells directly to shops. During January 20XX the following credit sales to customers took place:

Invoice No. 6237 to Hoppers Ltd £547 plus VAT
Invoice No. 6238 to Body Perfect £620 plus VAT
Invoice No. 6239 to Esporta Leisure £346 plus VAT
Invoice No. 6240 to Langans Beauty £228 plus VAT
Invoice No. 6241 to Body Perfect £548 plus VAT
Invoice No. 6242 to Superior Products £221 plus VAT
Invoice No. 6243 to Esporta Leisure £416 plus VAT
Invoice No. 6244 to Hoppers Ltd £238 plus VAT
Invoice No. 6245 to Langans Beauty £274 plus VAT

You are required to:

(a) **Enter these transactions into the sales day book given below.**

(b) **Cast the columns of the sales day book and check that they cross cast.**

Sales day book

Customer	Invoice number	Total £	VAT £	Net £

Cross-cast check:

	£
Net	
VAT	—
Total	═

....

Task 3.4

During January the following credit notes were issued by Natural Productions to various customers:

Credit note No. 1476 to Hoppers Ltd £68.70 plus VAT

Credit note No. 1477 to Esporta Leisure £89.20 plus VAT

Credit note No. 1478 to Superior Products £11.75 plus VAT

You are required to:

(a) **Enter these transactions into the sales returns day book given below.**

(b) **Cast the columns of the sales returns day book and check that they cross cast.**

Sales returns day book

Customer	Credit note number	Total £	VAT £	Net £

Cross-cast check:

	£
Net	
VAT	—
Total	=

Task 3.5

Natural Productions manufactures a variety of soaps and bath products. It buys materials for the manufacturing process from a number of suppliers on credit. It also buys other items such as stationery and packaging on credit. During January 20XX Natural Productions received the following invoices from credit suppliers:

4 Jan   Invoice No. 03576 from P J Phillips £357 plus VAT for materials
6 Jan   Invoice No. 18435 from Trenter Ltd £428 plus VAT for materials
9 Jan   Invoice No. 43654 from W J Jones £210 plus VAT for stationery
12 Jan   Invoice No. 03598 from P J Phillips £413 plus VAT for materials
16 Jan   Invoice No. 28423 from Packing Supplies £268 plus VAT for packaging
19 Jan   Invoice No. 18478 from Trenter Ltd £521 plus VAT for materials
20 Jan   Invoice No. 84335 from O & P Ltd £624 plus VAT for materials
24 Jan   Invoice No. 28444 from Packing Supplies £164 plus VAT for packaging
28 Jan   Invoice No. 18491 from Trenter Ltd £368 plus VAT for materials
31 Jan   Invoice No. 43681 from W J Jones £104 plus VAT for stationery

You are required to:

(a) **Enter these transactions in the purchases day book given below.**

(b) **Cast the columns of the purchases day book and check that they cross cast.**

Purchases day book

Date	Supplier	Invoice number	Total £	VAT £	Purchases (materials) £	Stationery £	Packaging £

Cross-cast check:

	£
Packaging	
Stationery	
Purchases (materials)	
VAT	
Total	

Task 3.6

During January Natural Productions received the following credit notes from suppliers in relation to the invoices set out in Task 3.5:

10 Jan Credit note No. 04216 from P J Phillips materials of £98 plus VAT
16 Jan Credit note No. CN 0643 from W J Jones stationery of £56 plus VAT
30 Jan Credit note No. CN 1102 from O & P Ltd materials of £124 plus VAT

You are required to:

(a) **Enter these transactions in the purchases returns day book given below.**

(b) **Cast the columns of the purchases returns day book and check that they cross cast.**

Purchases returns day book

Date	Supplier	Credit note number	Total £	VAT £	Purchases (materials) £	Stationery £	Packaging £

Cross-cast check:

	£
Packaging	
Stationery	
Purchases (materials)	
VAT	
Total	

Chapter 4 Recording credit sales

Task 4.1

Ken trades in exotic dress materials. A new customer has phoned up with an enquiry about buying some materials from Ken.

What should Ken send the customer?

✓	
	A delivery note
	A price list
	A goods received note
	A statement of account

Task 4.2

Ken wishes to analyse his sales so that he can distinguish between those made to UK customers and those from abroad.

What is the best way for him to do this?

✓	
	Analyse every invoice into a separate column of his analysed sales day book
	Allocate one of two sales codes to each invoice and use this to write up the invoices in the analysed sales day book
	Allocate invoice numbers on a randomised basis
	Use a different sequence of invoice numbers for each customer

Task 4.3

You work in the accounts department for Southfield Electrical and on your desk are three purchase orders received from customers today. The purchase orders have already been checked to the purchase quotations and the list prices are correct on each purchase order.

You also have on your desk the customer details file which gives you the following information about the three customers:

Customer name	Customer code	Trade discount	Settlement discount
Whitehill Superstores	SL 44	10%	4% – 10 days
Quinn Ltd	SL 04	15%	–
Harper & Sons	SL 26	10%	3% – 14 days

You are required to complete the three blank sales invoices given for each of these purchase orders.

The last sales invoice sent out was 57103. Today's date is 8 January 20XX. If no settlement discount is offered or taken then payment is due within 30 days.

PURCHASE ORDER

WHITEHILL SUPERSTORES
28 Whitehill Park
Benham DR6 5LM
Tel 0303446 Fax 0303447

To: Southfield Electrical
Industrial Estate
Benham DR6 2FF

Number: 32431

Date: 4 Jan 20XX

Delivery address: Whitehill Superstores
28, Whitehill Park
Benham DR6 5LM

Product code	Quantity	Description	Unit list price £
6060	8	Hosch Tumble Dryer	300.00

Authorised by: P. Williams   **Date:** 04/01/XX

PURCHASE ORDER

QUINN LTD
High Rocks Estate
Drenchley
DR22 6PQ
Tel 0310442 Fax 0310443

To: Southfield Electrical
    Industrial Estate
    Benham DR6 2FF

Number: 24316

Date: 5 Jan 20XX

Delivery address: As above

Product code	Quantity	Description	Unit list price £
3170	14	Temax Mixer	35.00

Authorised by: *J. P. Walters*   **Date:** *05/01/XX*

PURCHASE ORDER

HARPER & SONS
30/34 High Street
Benham DR6 4ST
Tel 0303419 Fax 0303464

To: Southfield Electrical
Industrial Estate
Benham DR6 2FF

Number: 04367

Date: 4 Jan 20XX

Delivery address: 30/34 High Street
Benham DR6 4ST

Product code	Quantity	Description	Unit list price £
6150	3	Hosch Washing Machine	260.00

Authorised by: *S. Stevens* **Date:** 5 Jan 20XX

INVOICE number				
Southfield Electrical, Industrial Estate, Benham DR6 2FF				
VAT registration:	0264 2274 49			
Date/tax point:				
Order number:				
Customer:	Whitehill Superstores			
Account number (customer code)				
Product code		Quantity	Unit amount £	Total £
Trade discount		%		
Net total				
VAT at 20%				
Total				
Settlement discount				%

INVOICE number			
Southfield Electrical, Industrial Estate, Benham DR6 2FF			
VAT registration:	0264 2274 49		
Date/tax point:			
Order number:			
Customer name:	Quinn Ltd		
Account number (customer code)			
Product code	Quantity	Unit amount £	Total £
Trade discount	%		
Net total			
VAT at 20%			
Total			
Settlement discount			%

INVOICE number	
Southfield Electrical, Industrial Estate, Benham DR6 2FF	
VAT registration:	0264 2274 49
Date/tax point:	
Order number:	
Customer:	Harper & Sons
Account number (customer code)	

Product code	Quantity	Unit amount £	Total £
Trade discount	%		
Net total			
VAT at 20%			
Total			
Settlement discount			%

Task 4.4

You work in the accounts department of Whitehill Superstores. Given below are a purchase order and related delivery note and sales invoice in respect of a purchase of goods from Southfield Electrical.

You are required to check the documents carefully and note any problems that you discover, stating how you would deal with them.

PURCHASE ORDER

WHITEHILL SUPERSTORES
28 Whitehill Park
Benham DR6 5LM
Tel 0303446 Fax 0303447

To: Southfield Electrical
Industrial Estate
Benham
DR6 2FF

Number: 32202

Date: 16 Oct 20XX

Delivery address: Whitehill Superstores
28, Whitehill Park
Benham DR6 5LM

Product code	Quantity	Description	Unit list price £
7460	11	Magifen Vacuum	210.00
3264	7	Temax Food Processor	65.00
9406	15	Kensharp Toaster	15.00

Authorised by: *P. Winterbottom*   **Date:** 16 Oct 20XX

DELIVERY NOTE

Southfield Electrical
Industrial Estate
Benham DR6 2FF
Tel 0303379 Fax 0303152

Delivery address:

Whitehill Superstores
28, Whitehill Park
Benham DR6 5LM

Number: 34816
Date: 18 Oct 20XX
Order number: 32202

Product code	Quantity	Description
3264	7	Temax Food Processor
9406	12	Kensharp Toaster
7460	11	Magifen Vacuum

Received by: [Signature] *J. Jones*   **Print name:** J. Jones

Date: 18 Oct 20XX

INVOICE

Southfield Electrical
Industrial Estate
Benham DR6 2FF
Tel 0303379 Fax 0303152
VAT Reg 0264 2274 49

To: Whitehill Superstores
28, Whitehill Park
Benham DR6 5LM

Invoice number: 56501

Date/tax point: 22 Oct 20XX

Order number: 32202

Account number: SL 44

Quantity	Description	Stock code	Unit amount £	Total £
7	Temax Food Processor	3264	65.00	455.00
15	Kensharp Toaster	9406	15.00	225.00
11	Magifen Vacuum	7460	220.00	2,420.00
				3,100.00
Less:	10% discount			310.00

Net total	2,790.00
VAT	535.68
Invoice total	3,325.68

Terms
4% discount for settlement within 10 days of invoice date, otherwise net 30 days
E & OE
Carriage Paid

Task 4.5

Given below is a credit note for a customer which receives 20% trade discount.

You are required to check it carefully, state what is wrong with it and calculate the correct figures. Remember that VAT must be rounded down to the nearest penny, though other figures may be rounded up to the nearest penny if appropriate.

CREDIT NOTE

SOUTHFIELD ELECTRICAL
INDUSTRIAL ESTATE
Benham DR6 2FF
Tel 0303379 Fax 0303152
VAT Reg 0264 2274 49

To:

B. B. Berry Ltd
Industrial Estate
Benham
DR6 5FW

Credit note number: 08669
Date/tax point: 22 Oct 20XX
Order number 40102
Account number: 5416

Quantity	Description	Stock code	Unit amount	Total
			£	£
3	Zanpoint fridge	4770	220.00	660.00
2	Temax whisk	3212	6.99	19.38
			Net total	679.38
			VAT	135.88
			Gross total	543.50

Reason for credit note:

Goods not ordered

Task 4.6

You work in the accounts department of Southfield Electrical. You have been given the two credit notes below. You are told that settlement discount is not relevant to the calculations on them.

You are required to:

(a) **Use the credit notes to write up the sales returns day book.**

(b) **Total the sales returns day book.**

Sales returns day book

Date	Customer	Credit note number	Customer code	Gross total £	VAT £	Net £
	Totals					

CREDIT NOTE

SOUTHFIELD ELECTRICAL
INDUSTRIAL ESTATE
Benham DR6 2FF
Tel 0303379 Fax 0303152
VAT Reg 0264 2274 49

Invoice to:
Whitehill Superstores
28 Whitehill Park
Benham DR6 5LM

Credit note number: 08650
Date/tax point: 21 Sept 20XX
Order number 6021
Account number: SL 44

Quantity	Description	Stock code	Unit amount £	Total £
1	Zanpoint Fridge	3676	330.00	330.00
Less:	10% discount			33.00

Net total	297.00
VAT	59.40
Gross total	356.40

Reason for credit note:
Damaged goods

25

CREDIT NOTE

SOUTHFIELD ELECTRICAL
INDUSTRIAL ESTATE
Benham DR6 2FF
Tel 0303379 Fax 0303152
VAT Reg 0264 2274 49

Invoice to:

    Dagwell Enterprises
    Dagwell House
    Hopchurch Rd
    Winnish
    DR2 6LT

Credit note number: 08651
Date/tax point: 23 Sept 20XX
Order number 5983
Account number: SL 15

Quantity	Description	Stock code	Unit amount	Total
			£	£
6	Temax Coffee maker	6470	40.00	240.00
Less:	15% discount			36.00

Net total	204.00
VAT	40.80
Gross total	244.80

Reason for credit note:

Goods not ordered

Task 4.7

You work in the accounts department of Southfield Electrical. The following are extracts from the day books relating to transactions in May 20XX with Alpha Services & Co. together with a remittance advice note for a cheque payment received in May 20XX from the customer.

You are required to enter the transactions in the sales ledger and prepare a statement of account for Alpha Services as at the end of May 20XX.

Sales day book – extract

Date 20XX	Customer	Invoice number	Customer code	Total £	VAT £	Net £
7 May	Alpha Services	715	SL10	5,190.00	865.00	4,325.00
17 May	Alpha Services	787	SL10	10,020.00	1,670.00	8,350.00

Sales returns day book – extract

Date 20XX	Customer	Credit note number	Customer code	Total £	VAT £	Net £
12 May	Alpha Services	551	SL10	624.00	104.00	520.00

REMITTANCE ADVICE NOTE	Remittance advice note number 013278
Alpha Services	
83 Abbey Road	
Durringham DU5 2WP	
Supplier:	**Southfield Electrical**
	Industrial Estate
	Benham DR6 2FF
Account number (supplier code)	**PL 821**

Date	Transaction reference	Amount £
21/04/XX	Invoice 600	289.50
27/04/XX	Credit note 401	(35.87)
1/5/XX	Payment made – cheque enclosed	253.63

Sales ledger

| Alpha Services | | | SL 10 |

Details	£	Details	£
Balance b/d	253.63		

STATEMENT OF ACCOUNT				
Southfield Electrical				
Industrial Estate				
Benham DR6 2FF				
Tel: 01239 345639				
VAT registration:		0264 2274 49		
Date:				
Customer:		Alpha Services 83 Abbey Road Durringham DU5 2WP		
Account number (customer code)				
Date	**Details**	**Debit £**	**Credit £**	**Balance £**
Amount now due				

Task 4.8

Given below are the details of two cheques received by Southfield Electrical, today 20 November 20XX, together with extracts from the sales invoices that are being paid in each case.

Check that the correct amount has been paid and if not explain where the error has been made.

Cheques received:

Cheque from Hayworth Ltd for £516.09

Cheque from Harper & Sons for £709.48

Invoice number	30227	
Date:	7 November 20XX	
To:	Hayworth Ltd	
		£
Goods value		448.00
VAT		86.01
Invoice total		534.01

4% settlement discount for payment received within 10 days of invoice date, otherwise 30 days net

Invoice number	30256	
Date:	12 November XX	
To:	Harper & Sons	
		£
Goods value		620.00
VAT		119.04
Invoice total		739.04

4% settlement discount for payment received within 10 days of invoice date, otherwise 30 days net

Chapter 5 Recording credit purchases

Task 5.1

Ken trades in exotic dress materials.

Complete the following statement:

When a supplier delivers materials to him he retains the supplier's delivery note and also prepares [   ] once he has had a chance to inspect the quality of the items.

Picklist:

An invoice

A goods received note

A remittance advice

Task 5.2

Complete the following statement:

A code which will help Ken to classify the different types of material purchase when completing his analysed purchases day book is

✓	
	A supplier code
	A product code

Task 5.3

Ken has been offered a settlement discount by one of his suppliers of '2% for payment within 10 days'. He receives an invoice dated 10 June on 12 June with a total of £239.20, which includes VAT of £39.20. He wishes to take advantage of the discount.

(a) **By what date must the supplier receive the payment?**

[   ]

(b) **How much should Ken pay the supplier on that date?**

£ [   ]

Task 5.4

You work for Newmans, a music shop, in the accounts department and one of your responsibilities is to organise the payments to suppliers. You have been off sick for the last week and a half and therefore it is urgent that you consider the invoices that are on your desk requiring payment.

Newmans' policy is to pay any invoices that are due each Friday. When a cheque is written on a Friday it does not then reach the supplier until Monday, ie three days later. If a settlement discount is offered by a supplier then this is taken if the discount will still be valid on the Monday. Otherwise the policy is to take the maximum amount of credit available.

Today's date is Friday 27 January 20XX. Thereafter, the following payment dates are 3 February, 10 February and 17 February. Remember that, as payments take three days to reach the supplier, any invoice dated earlier than 7 January with a 30-day period must be paid today, because if they are delayed until 3 February then the payments will not be received until 6 February, more than 30 days after they are due.

The invoices that are on your desk are scheduled below:

Invoice date	Supplier name	Terms	Total £	VAT £	Net £
5 Jan	Henson Press	30 days	336.00	56.00	280.00
8 Jan	GH Publications	30 days	136.80	22.80	114.00
12 Jan	Ely Instruments	20 days 2% discount otherwise 30 days	765.44	125.44	640.00
15 Jan	Hams Instruments	14 days 2.5% discount otherwise 30 days	370.45	60.45	310.00
19 Jan	CD Supplies	10 days 3% discount otherwise 30 days	138.02	22.42	115.60
22 Jan	Jester Press	10 days 3.5% discount otherwise 30 days	152.22	24.62	127.60
22 Jan	Henson Press	30 days	306.00	51.00	255.00
23 Jan	CD Supplies	10 days 3% discount otherwise 30 days	78.08	12.68	65.40
25 Jan	Jester Press	10 days 3.5% discount otherwise 30 days	47.12	7.62	39.50
25 Jan	Buser Ltd	7 days 5% discount otherwise 30 days	291.55	46.55	245.00

In the schedule given below show the date that each invoice should be paid and the amount for which the cheque should be written out.

Invoice date	Supplier name	Payment date	Working	Amount of cheque £
5 Jan	Henson Press			
8 Jan	GH Publications			
12 Jan	Ely Instruments			
15 Jan	Hams Instruments			
19 Jan	CD Supplies			
22 Jan	Jester Press			
22 Jan	Henson Press			
23 Jan	CD Supplies			
25 Jan	Jester Press			
25 Jan	Buser Ltd			

Task 5.5

Given below is a statement received by your organisation, Edgehill Designs, from one of its credit suppliers, P T Supplies, as at 31 January 20XX. You are instructed to pay all of the invoices less credit notes up to 10 January. Today's date is 7 February.

You are required to complete the remittance advice attached to the statement. Note that this supplier does not offer a settlement discount to your organisation.

STATEMENT

P.T. Supplies
28 Farm Court Road
Drenchley DR22 4XT

To: ⌐ Edgehill Designs ⌐   **Account number:** SL 53

Date: 31 January 20XX

Date	Details	Debit	Credit	Balance
1 Jan	Balance b/f	227.63		227.63
6 Jan	Inv 20671	107.22		334.85
8 Jan	Inv 20692	157.63		492.48
9 Jan	Payment - Thank you		227.63	264.85
10 Jan	CN 04722		28.41	236.44
17 Jan	Inv 20718	120.48		356.92
25 Jan	Inv 20734	106.18		463.10
30 Jan	CN 04786		16.15	446.95

Amount now due | £446.95 |

REMITTANCE ADVICE

To: P.T. Supplies   From: Edgehill Designs
28 Farm Court Road
Drenchley DR22 4XT

                              Date:

Reference	Amount £	Paid ✓

CHEQUE ENCLOSED

Task 5.6

Given below is an invoice received by Whitehill Superstores. You are also given the related purchase order, delivery note and goods received note.

You are required to check the invoice thoroughly and note any problems that you discover.

GOODS RECEIVED NOTE

Supplier: Southfield Electrical

GRN number: 47422

Date: 16 Sept 20XX

Order number: 32103

Delivery Note No: 34660

Quantity	Description	Stock code
10	A3 Night Light	9116
6	Zanpoint Tumble Dryer	4560

Received by: L Daniels

Checked by: D Richards

Comments: All in good condition

DELIVERY NOTE

Southfield Electrical
Industrial Estate
Benham DR6 2FF
Tel 0303379 Fax 0303152

Delivery address:

Whitehill Superstores
28, Whitehill Park
Benham DR6 5LM

Number: 34660
Date: 15 Sept 20XX
Order number: 32103

Product code	Quantity	Description
9116	10	A3 Night Light
4560	6	Zanpoint Tumble Dryer

Received by: [Signature] *L Daniels* **Print name:** L Daniels

Date: 15 Sept 20XX

PURCHASE ORDER

WHITEHILL SUPERSTORES
28 Whitehill Park
Benham DR6 5LM
Tel 0303446 Fax 0303447

To: Southfield Electrical
Industrial Estate
Benham
DR6 2FF

Number: 32103
Date: 10 Sept 20XX

Delivery address: As above

Product code	Quantity	Description	Price
4560	7	Zanpoint Tumble Dryer	245.00
9116	10	A3 Night light	24.58

Authorised by: *P. Winterbottom* **Date:** 10 Sept 20XX

INVOICE

Southfield Electrical
Industrial Estate
Benham DR6 2FF
Tel 0303379 Fax 0303152
VAT Reg 0264 2274 49

To:
Whitehill Superstores
28, Whitehill Park
Benham DR6 5LM

Invoice number: 56389

Date/tax point: 2 Oct 20XX

Order number: 32103

Account number: SL 44

Quantity	Description	Stock code	Unit amount £	Total £
7	Zanpoint Tumble Dryer	4560	245.00	1,778.00
10	A3 Night lights	9116	24.58	245.80
				2023.80
Less:	10% discount			202.38

Net total	1,821.42
VAT	364.28
Invoice total	2,185.70

Terms
4% discount for settlement within 10 days, otherwise 30 days net
E & OE
Carriage paid

BPP
LEARNING MEDIA

Task 5.7

Given below is an invoice received by Dartmouth Supplies and the related purchase order and delivery note. The supplier's file shows that a 10% trade discount is normally given but no settlement discount is offered.

You are required to check this invoice thoroughly and to note any problems that you discover.

INVOICE

Dan Industrials
Park Rise
Fenbridge DR2 7AD
Tel 0461222 Fax 461223
VAT Reg 0621 3384 20

To: Dartmouth Supplies
Fenbridge Estate North
Fenbridge
DR2 6PQ

Invoice number: 77412

Date/tax point: 7 Oct 20XX

Order number: 317428

Account number: SL 116

Quantity	Description	Stock code	Unit amount £	Total £
24	Regent Chair	C11	40.50	972.00
16	Imperial Desk	D46	96.00	1,536.00

Net total	2,535.00
VAT	507.00
Invoice total	3,042.00

Terms
Net 30 days
E & OE

PURCHASE ORDER

DARTMOUTH SUPPLIES
Fenbridge Estate North
Fenbridge DR2 6PQ
Tel 0461310 Fax 0461311

To: Dan Industrials
Park Rise
Fenbridge
DR2 7AD

Number: 317428

Date: 20 Sept 20XX

Delivery address: As above

Product code	Quantity	Description	Price (£)
D46	16	Imperial Desk	96.00
C11	24	Regent Chair	40.50

Authorised by: J. Sellers   **Date:** 20 Sept 20XX

DELIVERY NOTE

Dan Industrials
Park Rise
Fenbridge DR2 7AD
Tel 0461222 Fax 461223

Delivery address:

Dartmouth Supplies
Fenbridge Estate North
Fenbridge
DR2 6PQ

Number: 62601
Date: 27 Sept 20XX
Order number: 317428

Product code	Quantity	Description
D46	16	Imperial Desk
C11	24	Regent Chair

Received by: [Signature] S Simons   **Print name:** S Simons

Date: 27 Sept 20XX

Task 5.8

You have been given an extract from your organisation's purchases day book in respect of credit transactions taking place in June. No entries have yet been made in the ledgers.

Information from the suppliers' files indicate that Seashell Ltd offers a 10% settlement discount for payment within 10 days. Opal & Co does not offer a settlement discount. Both suppliers charge VAT on sales.

You are required to complete the purchases day book and state what the entries will be in the purchases ledger.

Purchases day book

Date 20XX	Details	Invoice number	Total £	VAT £	Net £
30 June	Seashell Ltd	8971	2568.80	642.20	3,211.00
30 June	Opal & Co	05119	4,800.00	960	3840
	Totals		7368.80	1332.20	7051

Purchases ledger

Account name	Amount £	Debit ✓	Credit ✓
Seashell ▼	2568.80		✓
Opal & Co ▼	4800		✓

Picklist:

Seashell Ltd
Opal & Co
Net
Purchases
Purchases ledger control
Purchases returns
Sales
Sales ledger control
Sales returns
Total
VAT

Task 5.9

You work for Bailie Ltd. Shown below is a statement of account received from a credit supplier, Dazzle Ltd, and the supplier's account as shown in the purchases ledger of Bailie Ltd.

Dazzle Ltd
21 Albert Street
Keeley
KE4 7AB

To: Bailie Ltd
5 Purley Road
Keeley
KE5 7LW

STATEMENT OF ACCOUNT

Date 20XX	Reference	Details	Debit £	Credit £	Balance £
1 July	8371	Goods	335		335
3 July	8412	Goods	420		755
7 July	8515	Goods	723		1,478
10 July	CN 3215	Goods returned		250	1,228
16 July		Cheque		485	743

Purchases ledger – Dazzle Ltd

Date 20XX	Details	Amount £	Date 20XX	Details	Amount £
15 July	Bank – cheque	485	1 July	PDB 8371	335
15 July	Discount received	20	3 July	PDB 8412	420
			7 July	PDB 8515	723

(a) **Which item is missing from the statement of account from Dazzle Ltd?**

(b) **Which item is missing from the supplier account in Bailie Ltd's purchases ledger?**

(c) **Assuming any differences between the statement of account from Dazzle Ltd and the supplier account in Bailie Ltd's purchases ledger are simply due to omission errors, what is the amount owing to Dazzle Ltd?**

£	99

Task 5.10

A supply of nails has been delivered to Acute Carpentry by Carbon Irons. The purchase order sent from Acute Carpentry, and the invoice from Carbon Irons, are shown below.

Acute Carpentry

Purchase Order No. 78639

To: Carbon Irons

Date: 16 June

Please supply 30 boxes 6" nails product code N1106
Purchase price: £20 per box, plus VAT
Discount: less 10% trade discount, as agreed.

Carbon Irons

Invoice No. 2318

Acute Carpentry

18 June

30 .... boxes product code N1106 @ £25 each	£750.00
VAT @ 20%	£150.00
Total	£900.00

Terms: 30 days net

Check the invoice against the purchase order and answer the following questions.

	Yes ✓	No ✓
Has the correct purchase price of the cardboard boxes been charged?		✓
Has the correct discount been applied?		✓
What would be the VAT amount charged if the invoice was correct?	£	
What would be the total amount charged if the invoice was correct?	£	675

Task 5.11

Ken runs a business trading in exotic dress materials. He sends out cheques to suppliers on the last day of the month following the month of invoice. Below is an extract from Ken's purchases ledger for his supplier, Mack Materials.

Mack Materials

Date 20XX	Details	Amount £	Date 20XX	Details	Amount £
31 May	Bank	890	1 May	Balance b/d	890
19 May	Purchases returns Credit note 43	31	7 May	Purchases Invoice 901	760
			3 June	Purchases Invoice 963	189

(a) **Complete the remittance advice note below.**

Ken's Exotics
1 Bath Street
Cembury, CE11 9SD

REMITTANCE ADVICE

To: Mack Materials   Date: 30 June 20XX

Please find attached our cheque in payment of the following amounts.

Invoice number	Credit note number	Amount £
901		760
	43	31
Total amount paid		729

(b) **Which of the following statements is true?**

	✓
The remittance advice note will be sent to the accounts department at Mack Materials to request that a cheque is raised	
The remittance advice note will be sent to Mack Materials' bank to advise them of the amount being paid	
The remittance advice note will be sent to the customer to advise them of the amount being paid	
The remittance advice note will be sent to the supplier to advise them of the amount being paid	✓

Task 5.12

Ken has received a statement from a supplier which shows that, as at the end of June 20XX, he owes the supplier £2,876. The purchases ledger account for this supplier shows that at that date Ken only owed £1,290.

Which of the following items would explain the difference?

	✓
Ken has requested a credit note from the supplier for £1,586 which he has not yet received	
Ken sent a cheque for £1,586 to the supplier on 30 June 20XX	
Ken ordered some items from the supplier on 30 June for £1,586 but the goods have not yet been delivered and an invoice has not yet been raised	

Chapter 6 Double entry bookkeeping

Task 6.1

Identify whether each of the following is an asset or a liability:

	Asset ✓	Liability ✓
A trade receivable		
A car used in the business		
A loan from the bank		
A bank overdraft		
Cash in hand		
VAT owed to HMRC		
A trade payable		
Inventory of raw materials		

Task 6.2

Complete the following statements using the word 'debit' or 'credit' in each case:

An increase in an expense is a [   ]

A decrease in a liability is a [   ]

An increase in income is a [   ]

An increase in an asset is a [   ]

An increase in capital is a [   ]

A decrease in an asset is a [   ]

An increase in a liability is a [   ]

A decrease in capital is a [   ]

Task 6.3

State the two effects of each of these transactions in the space given below.

(i)   James paid £20,000 into a business bank account in order to start the business.

Effect 1	Effect 2
increase in cash	increase capital

(ii)   He paid an initial rental of £2,500 by cheque for the shop that he is to trade from.

Effect 1	Effect 2
decrease in cash	

(iii)   He purchased a van by cheque for £7,400.

Effect 1	Effect 2

(iv)   He purchased £6,000 of goods for resale on credit.

Effect 1	Effect 2

(v)   He sold goods for £1,000 – the customer paid by cheque.

Effect 1	Effect 2

(vi)   He sold goods on credit for £4,800.

Effect 1	Effect 2

(vii)   He paid shop assistants' wages by cheque totalling £2,100.

Effect 1	Effect 2

(viii)   He made further sales on credit for £3,900.

Effect 1	Effect 2

(ix)   He purchased a further £1,400 of goods for resale by cheque.

Effect 1	Effect 2

(x)   £3,700 was received from credit customers.

Effect 1	Effect 2

(xi)   He paid £3,300 to credit suppliers.

Effect 1	Effect 2

(xii)   He withdrew £800 from the business for his living expenses.

Effect 1	Effect 2

Task 6.4

Using the information above about James's early transactions, enter them into the given ledger accounts.

Bank

Details	£	Details	£

Capital

Details	£	Details	£

Rent

Details	£	Details	£

Van

Details	£	Details	£

Purchases

Details	£	Details	£

Purchases ledger control

Details	£	Details	£

Sales account

Details	£	Details	£

Sales ledger control

Details	£	Details	£

Wages

Details	£	Details	£

Drawings

Details	£	Details	£

Task 6.5

What is the double entry required for discounts allowed to customers?

	Debit ✓	Credit ✓
Discounts allowed		
Sales ledger control		

Task 6.6

Given below are two credit customers' accounts.

You are required to find the balance carried down on each account.

T N Designs			
	£		£
1 May balance b/d	2,643.56	8 May CB	1,473.28
11 May SDB – 27491	828.40	24 May SRDB Cn0381	256.89
18 May SDB – 27513	1,088.65		

Harold & partners			
	£		£
1 May balance b/d	1,367.83	7 MAY CB	635.78
5 May SDB – 27465	998.20	7 May CB – discount	33.46
12 May SDB – 27499	478.92	15 May SRDB – Cn0364	106.34
20 May SDB – 27524	258.28	30 May CB	663.66
		30 May CB – discount	34.93

Task 6.7

A payment is made to a supplier for £367.48 after a settlement discount of £12.50 has been taken.

What is the double entry for this transaction?

Account name	Debit £	Credit £
P CLA C		367.48
Bank	367.48	
P CLA	12.50	
Discount receiv		12.50

Task 6.8

For each of the following, indicate whether they are capital or revenue transactions:

	Capital ✓	Revenue ✓
Purchase of a new computer paid for by cheque		
Purchase of printer paper by cheque		
Purchase of a new business car on credit		
Payment of road tax on a new business car		
Payment of rent for the business premises		

Task 6.9

Calculate the balance on the following ledger accounts and bring them down, including appropriate dates, details and amounts.

Purchases ledger control

Date	Details	£	Date	Details	£
31 Oct	Purchases returns	4,467	1 Oct	Balance b/d	41,204
31 Oct	Bank	36,409	31 Oct	Purchases	52,390
31 Oct	Discounts received	125			

Petty cash

Date	Details	£	Date	Details	£
1 Oct	Balance b/d	200.00	31 Oct	Expenses	183.25
31 Oct	Bank	183.25			

VAT

Date	Details	£	Date	Details	£
31 Oct	Sales returns	40.00	1 Oct	Balance b/d	183.25
31 Oct	Purchases	1,900.00	31 Oct	Purchases returns	62.00
			31 Oct	Sales	3,250.00

Task 6.10

For each of the following, indicate whether they are capital or revenue transactions:

	Capital ✓	Revenue ✓
Payment of a credit supplier for goods received for resale		✓
Receipt of proceeds from sale of car used in the business	✓	
Payment of drawings to the business owner	✓	
Acquisition of new machine for use over five years	✓	
Payment by a cash customer for goods		✓

Chapter 7 Maintaining the Cash Book

Task 7.1

You work for Natural Productions and one of your duties is to write up the cash book. Most of the payments are to credit suppliers but there are some purchases of materials (which all include VAT) from small suppliers with which Natural Productions does not have a credit account.

Purchases in cash were made as follows:

Date	Amount including VAT
10 Jul	£415.80
11 Jul	£85.80
14 Jul	£107.52

The cheque payment listing for the week ending 14 July is given below:

Cheque Payment Listing

Date	Cheque number	Supplier	Amount £	Discount £
10 Jul	002156	W J Jones	521.36	10.50
11 Jul	002157	Trenter Ltd	358.65	
11 Jul	002158	Packing Supplies	754.36	26.30
12 Jul	002159	P J Phillips	231.98	
13 Jul	002160	O & P Ltd	721.30	17.56

You are required to:

(a) **Record these payments in the analysed cash book (credit side) given below.**

(b) **Total the cash book (credit side) and check that it cross-casts.**

Cash book – credit side

Date	Details	Cheque no	Discounts received £	Cash £	Bank £	VAT £	Cash purchases £	Trade payables £

Cross-cast check:

	£
Trade payables	
Cash purchases	
VAT	
Total	
Cash	
Bank	
Total	

....

Task 7.2

Given below are the cheque stubs for the six payments made by Newmans on 27 January.

You have also looked at the standing order and direct debit instruction file and noted that there is a standing order due to be paid to the local council for business rates of £255.00 on the 27th of each month, and a direct debit for rent of £500.00 also due on 27th of the month.

You are required to write up the cash book (credit side) given below, total it and check that it cross-casts.

	Date	27 Jan 20XX
	Henson Press	
	£	329.00
		003014

	Date	27 Jan 20XX
	Ely Instruments	
	Discount 12.80	
	£	736.96
		003015

	Date	27 Jan 20XX
	Jester Press	
	Discount 4.47	
	£	144.67
		003016

	Date	27 Jan 20XX
	CD Supplies	
	Discount 1.96	
	£	74.54
		003017

	Date	27 Jan 20XX
	Jester Press	
	Discount 1.38	
	£	44.79
		003018

	Date	27 Jan 20XX
	Buser Ltd	
	Discount 12.25	
	£	273.48
		003019

Cash book – credit side

Date	Details	Cheque no	Discounts received £	Cash £	Bank £	VAT £	Trade payables £	Rent & rates £

Cross-cast check:

	£
Rent & rates	
Trade payables	
Total	
Cash	
Bank	
Total	

Task 7.3

You work for Natural Productions. One of your duties is to write up the cash book. Natural Productions makes sales on credit to a number of credit customers who pay by cheque, and also has some cash sales from a small retail outlet attached to the factory for which customers pay in notes and coin.

The list of receipts in the week ending 14 July is given below.

RECEIPTS	
10 Jul	£891.36 from Superior Products – settlement discount £32.56
11 Jul	£295.68 from Hoppers Ltd
11 Jul	£138.24 from cash sales including VAT
13 Jul	£542.97 from Body Perfect – settlement discount £21.45
13 Jul	£209.76 from cash sales including VAT
14 Jul	£958.45 from Esporta Leisure settlement discount £42.58
14 Jul	£84.48 from cash sales including VAT
14 Jul	£752.45 from Langans Beauty

You are required to:

(a) **Record these receipts in the analysed cash book (debit side) given below.**

(b) **Total the cash book (debit side) and check that it cross-casts.**

Cash book – debit side

Date	Details	Discounts allowed £	Cash £	Bank £	VAT £	Cash sales £	Trade receivables £

Cross-cast check:

	£
Trade receivables	
Cash sales	
VAT	
Total	
Cash	
Bank	
Total	

Task 7.4

There are five payments to be entered in Canlan Ltd's cash book.

Receipts from suppliers for Canlan Ltd's cash purchases

Supplier: Dubai Dreams Received cash with thanks for goods bought. Net £270 VAT £54 Total £324	**Supplier: Walter Enterprises** Received cash with thanks for goods bought. Net £190 VAT £38 Total £228	**Supplier: Sinead Reilly** Received cash with thanks for goods bought. Net £56 (No VAT)

Stubs from Canlan Ltd's cheque book

Payee: Sumatra Trading (Purchases ledger account PL026) £7,265 (Note: We have taken £35 settlement discount) Cheque number 093673	Payee: SHSK Co For stationery (Canlan Ltd has no credit account with this supplier) £378 including VAT Cheque number 093674

(a) **Enter the details of the three receipts from suppliers and two cheque book stubs into the credit side of the cash book shown below. Total each column.**

Cash book – credit side

Details	Discounts £	Cash £	Bank £	VAT £	Trade payables £	Cash purchases £	Stationery £
Balance b/f			236				
Dubai Dreams							
Walter Enterprises							
Sinead Reilly							
Sumatra Trading							
SHSK Co							
Total							

(b) There are two cheques from credit customers to be entered in the cash book:

Park Farm Stores   £2,576

Tristram Pale Ltd   £4,233 (this customer has taken a £25 discount)

Enter these details into the debit side of the cash book and total each column.

Cash book – debit side

Details	Discounts £	Cash £	Bank £	Trade receivables £
Balance b/f		1,228		
Park Farm Stores				
Tristram Pale Ltd				
Total				

(c) **Using your answers to (a) and (b) above, calculate the cash balance.**

£ [ ]

(d) **Using your answers to (a) and (b) above, calculate the bank balance.**

£

(e) **Is the bank balance calculated in (d) above a debit or credit balance?**

	✓
Debit	
Credit	

Task 7.5

There are five payments to be entered in Kitchen Kuts' cash book.

Receipts

Received cash with thanks for goods bought. From Kitchen Kuts, a customer without a credit account. Net £200 VAT £40 Total £240 B. Smithson Ltd	Received cash with thanks for goods bought. From Kitchen Kuts, a customer without a credit account. Net £160 VAT £32 Total £192 H Hamnet	Received cash with thanks for goods bought. From Kitchen Kuts, a customer without a credit account. Net £320 (No VAT) Renee Reid

Cheque book counterfoils

Tenon Ltd (Purchase ledger account TEN006) £3,600 (Note: Have taken £80 settlement discount) 000168	Vernon Motor Repairs (We have no credit account with this supplier) £48 including VAT 000169

(a) **Enter the details from the three receipts and two cheque book stubs into the credit side of the cash book shown below and total each column.**

Cash book – credit side

Details	Discount £	Cash £	Bank £	VAT £	Trade payables £	Cash purchases £	Motor expenses £
Balance b/f			16,942				
B Smithson Ltd							
H Hamnet							
Renee Reid							
Tenon Ltd							
Vernon Motor Repairs							
Total							

There are two cheques from credit customers to be entered in Kitchen Kuts' cash book:

G Brownlow   £749

S Barnett   £300 (this customer has taken a £30 discount)

(b) **Enter the above details into the debit side of the cash book and total each column.**

Cash book – debit side

Details	Discount £	Cash £	Bank £	Trade receivables £
Balance b/f		1,325		
G Brownlow				
S Barnett				
Total				

(c) **Using your answers to (a) and (b) above, calculate the cash balance.**

£ [ ]

(d)   **Using your answers to (a) and (b) above, calculate the bank balance.**

£	

(e)   **Will the bank balance calculated in (d) above be a debit or credit balance?**

	✓
Debit	
Credit	

Chapter 8 Double entry for sales and trade receivables

Task 8.1

James give you of the details of his sales on credit and cheque receipts from credit customers during the first month (January 20XX). James is registered for VAT and charges VAT on all sales. He does not offer any discounts for early settlement.

Sales:			
Customer	Customer code	Invoice number	Invoice total £
To H Simms	SL 45	0001	1,800
To P Good	SL 21	0002	3,000
To K Mitchell	SL 30	0003	912
To C Brown	SL 05	0004	2,790

Cheque receipts:	
Customer	£
From H Simms	900
From P Good	1,400
From K Mitchell	912
From C Brown	490

Record these transactions in the day books given and then post the day books to the general ledger accounts and the sales ledger.

Sales day book

Date 20XX	Customer	Invoice number	Customer code	Total £	VAT £	Net £

Cash book – debit side

Date	Details	Bank £	VAT £	Cash sales £	Trade receivables £

General ledger

Sales ledger control

Details	£	Details	£

Sales

Details	£	Details	£

VAT

Details	£	Details	£

Sales ledger

H Simms SL 45

Details	£	Details	£

P Good SL 21

Details	£	Details	£

K Mitchell SL 30

Details	£	Details	£

C Brown SL 05

Details	£	Details	£

Task 8.2

Natural Productions is a small business that manufactures a variety of soaps and bath products which it sells directly to shops.

You are required to:

(a) **Post the totals of the sales day book to the general ledger accounts given.**

(b) **Post the individual entries to the sales ledger.**

Sales day book

Date 20XX	Customer	Invoice number	Total £	VAT £	Net £
2 Jan	Hoppers Ltd	6237	656.40	109.40	547.00
5 Jan	Body Perfect	6238	744.00	124.00	620.00
6 Jan	Esporta Leisure	6239	415.20	69.20	346.00
9 Jan	Langans Beauty	6240	273.60	45.60	228.00
12 Jan	Body Perfect	6241	657.60	109.60	548.00
16 Jan	Superior Products	6242	265.20	44.20	221.00
18 Jan	Esporta Leisure	6243	499.20	83.20	416.00
23 Jan	Hoppers Ltd	6244	285.60	47.60	238.00
26 Jan	Langans Beauty	6245	328.80	54.80	274.00
			4,125.60	687.60	3,438.00

(a) **General ledger**

Sales ledger control

Details	£	Details	£

VAT

Details	£	Details	£

Sales

Details	£	Details	£

(b)   **Sales ledger**

Hoppers Ltd

Details	£	Details	£

Body Perfect

Details	£	Details	£

Esporta Leisure

Details	£	Details	£

Langans Beauty

Details	£	Details	£

Superior Products

Details	£	Details	£

Task 8.3

Given below are four sales invoices sent out by Short Furniture, a business that manufactures wooden garden furniture for sale to retail outlets. These are the only invoices that have been issued this week.

You are required to:

(a) **Enter the invoices into the sales day book given.**

(b) **Total and check the sales day book.**

(c) **Post the sales day book to the general ledger and the sales ledger.**

INVOICE

Short Furniture
Eridge Estate
Benham DR6 4QQ
Tel 0303312 Fax 0303300
VAT Reg 0361 3282 60

To: Rocks Garden Suppliers
14 Windmill Lane
Benham

Invoice number: 08663

Date/tax point: 5 Jan 20XX

Order number: 4513

Account number: SL 22

Quantity	Description	Stock code	Unit amount £	Total £
2	6 Seat Dining Table	DT613	344.00	688.00
	Trade Discount			103.20

Net total		584.80
VAT		116.96
Invoice total		701.76

Terms
Net 30 days
E & OE

INVOICE

Short Furniture
Eridge Estate
Benham DR6 4QQ
Tel 0303312 Fax 0303300
VAT Reg 0361 3282 60

To: Eridge Nurseries
Eridge Estate
Benham

Invoice number: 08664

Date/tax point: 7 Jan 20XX

Order number: 61735F

Account number: SL 07

Quantity	Description	Stock code	Unit amount £	Total £
15	Plant Stands	PL006	23.85	357.75

Net total	357.75
VAT	71.55
Invoice total	429.30

Terms
Net 30 days
E & OE

INVOICE

Short Furniture
Eridge Estate
Benham DR6 4QQ
Tel 0303312 Fax 0303300
VAT Reg 0361 3282 60

To: Abergaven Garden Centre
Drenchley

Invoice number: 08665

Date/tax point: 7 Jan 20XX

Order number: S129

Account number: SL 16

Quantity	Description	Stock code	Unit amount £	Total £
3	Lounger Chairs	LC400	285.00	855.00
	Trade discount			85.50

Net total	769.50
VAT	153.90
Invoice total	923.40

Terms
Net 30 days
E & OE

INVOICE

Short Furniture
Eridge Estate
Benham DR6 4QQ
Tel 0303312 Fax 0303300
VAT Reg 0361 3282 60

To: Rother Nurseries
Rother Road
Benham

Invoice number: 08666

Date/tax point: 9 Jan 20XX

Order number: 06112

Account number: SL 13

Quantity	Description	Stock code	Unit amount £	Total £
2	Coffee Table	CT002	96.00	192.00
6	Dining Chairs	DC416	73.00	438.00
		Net total		630.00
		VAT		126.00
		Invoice total		756.00

Terms
Net 30 days
E & OE

(a) **Sales day book**

Customer	Invoice number	Customer code	Invoice total £	VAT £	Net £

(b) **Cross-cast check**

	£
Net	
VAT	——
Invoice total	══

(c) **General ledger**

Sales ledger control

Details	£	Details	£

VAT

Details	£	Details	£

Sales

Details	£	Details	£

Sales ledger

Eridge Nurseries SL 07

Details	£	Details	£

Rother Nurseries SL 13

Details	£	Details	£

Abergaven Garden Centre   SL 16

Details	£	Details	£

Rock Garden Suppliers   SL 22

Details	£	Details	£

Task 8.4

Returning to Natural Productions (see Task 8.2), during January the company issued some credit notes.

You are required to:

(a) **Post the totals of the sales returns day book to the general ledger accounts given.**

(b) **Post the individual entries to the sales ledger accounts used in the earlier task.**

Sales returns day book

Date 20XX	Customer	Invoice number	Total £	VAT £	Net £
17 Jan	Hoppers Ltd	1476	82.44	13.74	68.70
23 Jan	Esporta Leisure	1477	107.04	17.84	89.20
30 Jan	Superior Products	1478	14.16	2.36	11.80
			203.64	33.94	169.70

(a) **General ledger**

Sales ledger control

Details	£	Details	£
Sales	4,125.60		

VAT

Details	£	Details	£
		Sales	687.60

Sales returns

Details	£	Details	£
Sales			

(b) **Sales ledger**

Hoppers Ltd

Details	£	Details	£
SDB – 6237	656.40		
SDB – 6244	285.60		

Body Perfect

Details	£	Details	£
SDB – 6238	744.00		
SDB – 6241	657.60		

Esporta Leisure

Details	£	Details	£
SDB – 6239	415.20		
SDB – 6243	499.20		

Langans Beauty

Details	£	Details	£
SDB – 6240	273.60		
SDB – 6245	328.80		

Superior Products

Details	£	Details	£
SDB – 6242	265.20		

Task 8.5

Short Furniture has received the following remittance advices through the post in the week ending 7 February 20XX. The remittance advices from Rocks Garden Suppliers and Eridge Nurseries were the ones sent out by Short Furniture with the monthly statement. However, the remittance advices from Abergaven Garden Centre and Rother Nurseries were prepared by their accounts departments and must therefore be checked to their accounts in the sales ledger, which are given below.

Check each payment thoroughly and record any problems or comments in the table provided.

Sales ledger

	Rother Nurseries			SL 16
Date Details	£	Date Details		£
9 Jan SDB – 08666	756.00	20 Jan SRDB – 1470		96.50
16 Jan SDB – 08674	214.78			
24 Jan SDB – 08681	337.89			
5 Feb SDB – 08695	265.98			

	Abergaven Garden Centre		SL 17
Date Details	£	Date Details	£
7 Jan SDB – 08665	923.40		
13 Jan SDB – 08672	623.56		
26 Jan SDB – 08685	316.58		
3 Feb SDB – 08692	415.76		

	Comments
Payment from Rocks Garden Suppliers	
Payment from Eridge Nurseries	
Payment from Abergaven Garden Centre	
Payment from Rother Nurseries	

REMITTANCE ADVICE

To: Short Furniture
Eridge Estate
Benham DR6 4QQ
Tel 0303312 Fax 0303300

From: Rocks Garden Supplies

Date: 4 February 20XX

Reference	Amount £	Paid (✓)
08663	701.76	✓
1468	(343.57)	✓
08675	521.18	✓
08686	732.40	

CHEQUE ENCLOSED	£773.75

REMITTANCE ADVICE

To: Short Furniture
Eridge Estate
Benham DR6 4QQ
Tel 0303312 Fax 0303300

From: Eridge Nurseries

Date: 3 February 20XX

Reference	Amount £	Paid (✓)
08664	429.30	✓
08676	381.18	✓
1471	(206.23)	✓
08687	640.20	
08690	381.62	

CHEQUE ENCLOSED	£604.25

REMITTANCE ADVICE

To: Short Furniture
Eridge Estate
Benham DR6 4QQ
Tel 0303312 Fax 0303300

From: Abergaven Garden
Centre

Date: 4 February 20XX

Reference	Amount £	Paid (✓)
08665	923.40	✓
08672	623.56	✓
08685	316.58	✓

CHEQUE ENCLOSED	£1,863.54

REMITTANCE ADVICE

To: Short Furniture
Eridge Estate
Benham DR6 4QQ
Tel 0303312 Fax 0303300

From: Rother Nurseries

Date: 5 February 20XX

Reference	Amount £	Paid (✓)
08666	756.00	✓
08674	114.78	✓
1470	(96.50)	✓
08681	337.89	✓

CHEQUE ENCLOSED	**£1,112.17**

Task 8.6

Returning to Natural Productions (see Task 8.4) you are required to:

(a) Post the totals of receipts in the cash book to the general ledger accounts given below (note that in each case the discount was allowed to the customer after the invoice was prepared, and has been correctly calculated).

(b) Post each individual receipt from customers to their account in the sales ledger given below.

Date	Details	Discounts allowed £	Cash £	Bank £	VAT £	Cash sales £	Trade receivables £
23 Jan	Hoppers Ltd	20.00		553.96			553.96
23 Jan	Superior Products			116.70			116.70
24 Jan	Cash sales		131.16		21.86	109.30	
25 Jan	Esporta Leisure	11.36		367.20			367.20
27 Jan	Cash sales		88.56		14.76	73.80	
27 Jan	Body Perfect	21.86		706.64			706.64
27 Jan	Cash sales		60.12		10.02	50.10	
____	Langans Beauty	____		273.60	____	____	273.60
		53.22	279.84	2,018.10	46.64	233.20	2,018.10

General ledger

Cash

Details	£	Details	£

Bank

Details	£	Details	£

Sales ledger control

Details	£	Details	£
Sales	4,125.60	Sales returns	203.64

Sales

Details	£	Details	£
		SLCA	3,438.00

VAT

Details	£	Details	£
Sales returns	33.94	Sales	687.60

Discounts allowed

Details	£	Details	£

Sales ledger

Hoppers Ltd

Details	£	Details	£
SDB – 6237	656.40	SRDB – 1476	82.44
SDB – 6244	285.60		

Body Perfect

Details	£		£
SDB – 6238	744.00		
SDB – 6241	657.60		

Esporta Leisure

Details	£	Details	£
SDB – 6239	415.20	SRDB – 1477	107.04
SDB – 6243	499.20		

Langans Beauty

Details	£	Details	£
SDB – 6240	273.60		
SDB – 6245	328.80		

Superior Products

Details	£	Details	£
SDB – 6242	265.20	SRDB – 1478	14.16

....

Task 8.7

Ken trades in exotic dress materials. The following is a summary of his transactions with Crowley Ltd, a new credit customer.

£627 re invoice 1540 of 15 September
£728 re invoice 1560 of 29 September
£46 re credit note 89 of 3 October
£1,209 re invoice 1580 of 10 October
Cheque for £581 received 15 October

Complete the statement of account below.

Ken's Exotics
1 Bath Street
Cembury, CE11 9SD

To: Crowley Ltd   Date: 31 October 20XX

Date 20XX	Details	Transaction amount £	Outstanding amount £

....

Chapter 9 Double entry for purchases and trade payables

Task 9.1

For Natural Productions you are required to:

(a) Post the totals of the purchases day book to the general ledger accounts given.

(b) Post the individual entries to the purchases ledger accounts given.

Purchases day book

Date	Supplier	Invoice number	Total £	VAT £	Net £	Purchases £	Stationery £	Packaging £
4 Jan	P J Phillips	03576	428.40	71.40	357.00	357.00		
6 Jan	Trenter Ltd	18435	513.60	85.60	428.00	428.00		
9 Jan	W J Jones	43654	252.00	42.00	210.00		210.00	
12 Jan	P J Phillips	03598	495.60	82.60	413.00	413.00		
16 Jan	Packing Supplies	28423	321.60	53.60	268.00			268.00
19 Jan	Trenter Ltd	18478	625.20	104.20	521.00	521.00		
20 Jan	O & P Ltd	84335	748.80	124.80	624.00	624.00		
24 Jan	Packing Supplies	28444	196.80	32.80	164.00			164.00
28 Jan	Trenter Ltd	18491	441.60	73.60	368.00	368.00		
31 Jan	W J Jones	43681	124.80	20.80	104.00		104.00	
			4,148.40	691.40	3,457.00	2,711.00	314.00	432.00

General ledger

Purchases ledger control

Details	£	Details	£

VAT

Details	£	Details	£

Purchases

Details	£	Details	£

Stationery

Details	£	Details	£

Packaging

Details	£	Details	£

Purchases ledger

P J Phillips

Details	£	Details	£

Trenter Ltd

Details	£	Details	£

O & P Ltd

Details	£	Details	£

W J Jones

Details	£	Details	£

Packing Supplies

Details	£	Details	£

Task 9.2

Given below are the only four purchase invoices received by Short Furniture in the week ending 27 January 20XX. You are also given an extract from the supplier codes listing.

27 Jan Invoice No. 09642 from Ephraim Supplies £291.00 plus VAT for wood
27 Jan Invoice No. 06932 from Cavendish Woods £705.10 plus VAT for wood
27 Jan Invoice No. 67671 from Calverley Bros £145.60 plus VAT for polish
27 Jan Invoice No. 36004 from Culverden & Co £57.40 plus VAT for other purchases

Supplier codes listing

Calverley Bros	PL03
Cavendish Woods	PL14
Culverden & Co	PL23
Ephraim Supplies	PL39

You are required to:

(a) **Enter the invoices in the purchases day book given – note that purchases are analysed into wood, polish and varnish and other.**

(b) **Total and check the purchases day book.**

(c) **Post the purchases day book totals to the general ledger accounts given.**

(d) **Post the individual entries in the purchases day book to the suppliers' accounts in the purchases ledger given below.**

Purchases day book

Date	Supplier	Invoice number	Supplier code	Total £	VAT £	Net £	Wood Purchases £	Polish/ varnish purchases £	Other purchases £

Cross cast check:

	£
Net	
VAT	
Total	

General ledger

Purchases ledger control

Details	£	Details	£

VAT

Details	£	Details	£

Wood purchases

Details	£	Details	£

Polish/varnish purchases

Details	£	Details	£

Other purchases

Details	£	Details	£

Purchases ledger

Carverley Bros   PL 03

Details	£	Details	£

Cavendish Woods   PL 14

Details	£	Details	£

Culverder & Co   PL 23

Details	£	Details	£

Ephraim Supplies   PL 39

Details	£	Details	£

Task 9.3

Returning to Natural Productions (see Task 9.1) you are required to:

(a) Post the totals of the purchases returns day book to the general ledger accounts given.

(b) Post the individual entries to the purchases ledger accounts also given below.

Purchases returns day book

Date	Supplier	Credit note number	Total £	VAT £	Net £	Purchases £	Stationery £	Packaging £
10 Jan	P J Phillips	04216	117.60	19.60	98.00	98.00		
16 Jan	W J Jones	CN0643	67.20	11.20	56.00		56.00	
30 Jan	O & P Ltd	CN1102	148.80	24.80	124.00	124.00		
			333.60	55.60	278.00	222.00	56.00	

General ledger

Purchases ledger control

Details	£	Details	£
		Purchases etc	4,148.40

VAT

Details	£	Details	£
Purchases etc	691.40		

Purchases returns

Details	£	Details	£

Stationery

Details	£	Details	£
PLCA	314.00		

Purchases ledger

P J Phillips

Details	£	Details	£
		PDB 03576	428.40
		PDB 03598	495.60

W J Jones

Details	£	Details	£
		PDB 43654	252.00
		PDB 43681	124.80

O & P Ltd

Details	£	Details	£
		PDB 84335	748.80

Task 9.4

You work for Natural Productions and one of your duties is to transfer data from the cash book to the ledgers. Most of the payments are to credit suppliers but there are some cash purchases of materials from small suppliers which include VAT.

You are required to:

(a) **Post the totals of the credit side of the cash book to the general ledger accounts given below.**

(b) **Post each of the individual payments to the suppliers' accounts in the purchases ledger given below.**

Cash book – credit side

Date	Details	Cheque No	Discounts received £	Cash £	Bank £	VAT £	Cash purchases £	Trade payables £
23 Jan	Trenter Ltd	002144	10.00		1,105.07			1,105.07
23 Jan	Cash purchase	002145		108.00		18.00	90.00	
24 Jan	W J Jones	002146			252.00			252.00
24 Jan	P J Phillips	002147			806.40			806.40
24 Jan	Cash purchase	002148		128.28		21.38	106.90	
25 Jan	Packing Supp	002149	5.00		309.90			309.90
26 Jan	O & P Ltd	002150	20.00		580.00			580.00
27 Jan	Cash purchase	002151		96.96		16.16	80.80	
			35.00	333.24	3,053.37	55.54	277.70	3,053.37

General ledger

Purchases ledger control

Details	£	Details	£
Purchases returns etc	333.60	Purchases etc	4,148.40

VAT

Details	£	Details	£
Purchases etc	691.40	Purchases returns etc	55.60

Purchases

Details	£	Details	£
PLCA	2,711.00		

Discounts received

Details	£	Details	£

Purchases ledger

P J Phillips

Details	£	Details	£
PRDB 04216	117.60	PDB 03576	428.40
		PDB 03598	495.60

Trenter Ltd

Details	£	Details	£
		PDB 18435	513.60
		PDB 18478	625.20
		PDB 18491	441.60

W J Jones

Details	£	Details	£
PRDB CN0643	67.20	PDB 43654	252.00
		PDB 43681	124.80

O & P Ltd

Details	£	Details	£
PRDB CN1102	148.80	PDB 84335	748.80

Packing Supplies

Details	£	Details	£
		PDB 28423	321.60
		PDB 28444	196.80

Task 9.5

Ken trades in exotic dress materials. He codes all purchase invoices with a supplier code AND a general ledger code. A selection of the codes used is given below.

Supplier	Supplier Code
Henderson Co	HEN562
Mack Materials	MAC930
Vinceroy Ltd	VIN234
Streamers	STR220
AVR Partners	AVR001
Product	General Ledger Code
Lace	GL501
Calico	GL502
Seersucker	GL503
Cambric	GL504
Velvet	GL505

This is an invoice received from a supplier.

Vinceroy Ltd
17 Fall Road, Agburton AG5 2WE
VAT Registration No. 783 2873 33

Invoice number: 892

Ken's Exotics 1 Bath Street Cembury, CE11 9SD	5 Feb 20XX
20 metres .... Velvet @ £7.00 per metre	£140.00
VAT @ 20%	£ 28.00
Total	£168.00

(a) **Select which codes would be used to code this invoice.**

Supplier account code	
General ledger code	

(b) **Why is it necessary to use a general ledger code?**

Picklist:

To help trace relevant accounts quickly and easily
To make sure the correct balances are calculated
To prevent fraud

Chapter 10 Accounting for petty cash

Task 10.1

Natural Productions has a petty cash system based on an imprest amount of £100 which is replenished weekly. On Friday 20 January the total of the vouchers in the petty cash box was £68.34.

How much cash is required to replenish the petty cash box?

£	

....

Task 10.2

Newmans, the music shop, has an imprest petty cash system based upon an imprest amount of £120.00. During the week ending 27 January the petty cash vouchers given below were presented, authorised and paid.

```
PETTY CASH VOUCHER

Number: 0721              Date: 23 Jan

Details                   Amount

Coffee                    3 - 99
                Net       3 - 99
                VAT         -
                Gross     3 - 99

Claimed by:      T. Richards
Authorised by:   J. Clarke
```

```
PETTY CASH VOUCHER

Number: 0726              Date: 27 Jan

Details                   Amount

Computer disks            9 - 35
                Net       9 - 35
                VAT       1 - 87
                Gross     11 - 22

Claimed by:      D. Player
Authorised by:   J. Clarke
```

PETTY CASH VOUCHER

Number: *0722*　　　　　Date: *23 Jan*

Details	Amount
10 Books Postage Stamps	24 - 00
Net	24 - 00
VAT	-
Gross	24 - 00

Claimed by:　　*D. Player*

Authorised by:　*J. Clarke*

PETTY CASH VOUCHER

Number: *0723*　　　　　Date: *24 Jan*

Details	Amount
Taxi fare	8 - 94
Net	8 - 94
VAT	1 - 78
Gross	10 - 72

Claimed by:　　*P. L. Newman*

Authorised by:　*J. Clarke*

PETTY CASH VOUCHER

Number: *0724*　　　　　Date: *24 Jan*

Details	Amount
Printer paper	2 - 99
Envelopes	2 - 95
Net	5 - 94
VAT	1 - 18
Gross	7 - 12

Claimed by:　　*T. Richards*

Authorised by:　*J. Clarke*

PETTY CASH VOUCHER

Number: *0725*   Date: *26 Jan*

Details		Amount
Train fare		*13 - 60*
	Net	*13 - 60*
	VAT	*-*
	Gross	*13 - 60*

Claimed by: *P. L. Newman*

Authorised by: *J. Clarke*

You are required to:

(a) **Write up the petty cash vouchers in the petty cash book.**

(b) **Total the petty cash book (credit side) and check that it cross-casts.**

Petty cash book

Debit side			Credit side								
Date	Details	Amount £	Date	Details	Voucher number	Total £	VAT £	Travel £	Post £	Stationery £	Office supplies £
22 Jan	Bal b/f	120.00									

Cross-cast check:

	£
Office supplies	
Stationery	
Postage	
Travel	
VAT	
Total	

Task 10.3

On the first day of every month cash is drawn from the bank to restore the petty cash imprest level to £75.

A summary of petty cash transactions during November is shown below:

Opening balance on 1 November	£22
Cash from bank on 1 November	£53
Expenditure during month	£16

(a) **What will be the amount required to restore the imprest level on 1 December?**

£ [   ]

(b) **Will the receipt from the bank on 1 December be a debit or credit entry in the petty cash book?**

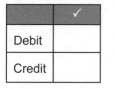

	✓
Debit	
Credit	

Task 10.4

Short Furniture has a monthly petty cash imprest system based upon an imprest amount of £150.00. During the month of January the following petty cash vouchers were authorised and paid:

Voucher No.	£
0473	12.60
0474	15.00
0475	19.75
0476	9.65
0477	10.00
0478	13.84
0479	4.26
0480	16.40

The cash in the petty cash box at 31 January was made up as follows:

£10 note	1
£5 note	4
£2 coin	3
£1 coin	7
50p coin	5
20p coin	8
10p coin	9
5p coin	4
2p coin	11
1p coin	8

(a) **Add together the voucher total and the petty cash in the box to arrive at the imprest amount at the end of January.**

	£
Voucher total	
Petty cash in the box	
Imprest amount	

(b) **The petty cash control account in the general ledger is given below. You are to balance the petty cash control account (this should be the same as the balance of cash in the petty cash box on 31 January).**

Petty cash control

		£			£
1 Jan	Balance b/f	150.00	31 Jan	Expenditure	101.50

Task 10.5

A business which is not registered for VAT has partially completed its petty cash book for November, as shown below.

Petty cash book

Debit side			Credit side					
Date	Details	Amount	Date	Details	Total	Stationery	Postage	Motor fuel
		£			£	£	£	£
1 Nov	Bal b/f	100	7 Nov	Postage stamps	20			
			15 Nov	Pens & pencils	18			
			22 Nov	Petrol	10			
			30 Nov	Envelopes	15			
	Total			Total				

(a) **Complete the analysis columns for the four items purchased from petty cash.**

(b) **Total and balance the petty cash book, showing clearly the balance carried down at 30 November.**

(c) **Enter the balance brought down at 1 December, showing clearly the date, details, and amount. You do NOT need to restore the imprest amount.**

Task 10.6

This is a summary of petty cash payments made by your business.

Post Office paid	£30.00 (no VAT)
Window cleaning paid	£25.60 plus VAT
MegaBus Company paid	£29.50 (no VAT)

(a) **Enter the above transactions in the petty cash book.**

(b) **Total the petty cash book and show the balance carried down.**

Petty cash book

Debit side		Credit side					
Details	Amount £	Details	Amount £	VAT £	Postage £	Travel £	Cleaning £
Balance b/f	175.00						

Task 10.7

On 20 September the petty cash control account has a balance of £96.70. The cash in the petty cash box is checked and the following notes and coins are there.

Notes and coins	£
2 × £20 notes	40.00
3 × £10 notes	30.00
2 × £5 notes	10.00
1 × £2 coins	2.00
5 × £1 coins	5.00
7 × 50p coins	3.50
11 × 10p coins	1.10
2 × 5p coins	0.10

(a) **Reconcile the cash amount in the petty cash box with the balance on the petty cash control account.**

Amount in petty cash box	£	
Balance on petty cash control account	£	
Difference	£	

At the end of September the cash in the petty cash box was £9.76.

(b) **Complete the petty cash reimbursement document below to restore the imprest amount of £250.**

Petty cash reimbursement		
Date: 30.09.20XX		
Amount required to restore the cash in the petty cash box	£	

Task 10.8

This is a summary of petty cash payments made by Kitchen Kuts.

Tom's Taxi paid	£18.00 (no VAT)
Post Office paid	£30.00 (no VAT)
SMP Stationery paid	£36.00 plus VAT

(a) **Enter the above transactions, in the order in which they are shown, in the petty cash book below.**

(b) **Total the petty cash book and show the balance carried down.**

Petty cash book

Debit side		Credit side					
Details	Amount £	Details	Amount £	VAT £	Postage £	Travel £	Stationery £
Balance b/f	150.00						

Task 10.9

Part way through a month the petty cash control account had a balance of £120.00. The cash in the petty cash box was checked and the following notes and coins were there.

Notes and coins	£
3 × £20 notes	60.00
5 × £5 notes	25.00
17 × £1 coins	17.00
23 × 50p coins	11.50
16 × 10p coins	1.60
21 × 5p coins	1.05

(a) **Reconcile the cash amount in the petty cash box with the balance on the petty cash control account.**

Amount in petty cash box	£	
Balance on petty cash control account	£	
Difference	£	

At the end of the month the cash in the petty cash box was £3.45.

(b) **Complete the petty cash reimbursement document below to restore the imprest amount of £200.**

Petty cash reimbursement		
Date: 31.07.20XX		
Amount required to restore the cash in the petty cash box	£	

Task 10.10

Ken trades in exotic dress materials. The following is the credit side of Ken's Petty Cash Book, which acts only as a book of prime entry.

(a) What will be the FIVE entries in the general ledger?

Petty cash book – credit side

Details	Voucher number	Total £	VAT £	Office expenses £	Stationery £	Maintenance £
Tea, coffee and milk for office	1234	15.20		15.20		
Printer cartridge	1235	39.12	6.52		32.60	
Repair to fire extinguisher	1236	54.00	9.00			45.00
Totals		108.32	15.52	15.20	32.60	45.00

General ledger

Account name	Amount £	Debit ✓	Credit ✓

(b) Which entry would be omitted if Ken's Petty Cash Book operated as a general ledger account as well?

Chapter 11 Initial trial balance

Task 11.1

You are given the following account balances from the general ledger of your organisation.

Would each balance be a debit or a credit balance in the trial balance?

Ledger account	Balance	Debit ✓	Credit ✓
Sales	592,513		
Telephone	1,295		
Sales ledger control	52,375		
Wages	104,288		
Purchases returns	8,229		
Bank overdraft	17,339		
Purchases	372,589		
Drawings	71,604		
Sales returns	32,800		
Car	14,700		
Purchases ledger control	31,570		

Task 11.2

Given below is the list of ledger balances for your organisation at 31 January 20XX.

You are required to prepare a trial balance as at 31 January 20XX.

	£	Debit £	Credit £
Motor vehicles	76,800		
Office equipment	36,440		
Sales	285,600		
Purchases	196,800		
Bank (overdraft)	2,016		
Petty cash	36		
Capital	90,000		
Sales returns	5,640		
Purchases returns	4,320		
Sales ledger control	42,960		
Purchases ledger control	36,120		
VAT (owed to HMRC)	15,540		
Drawings	12,040		
Telephone	1,920		
Electricity	3,360		
Wages	74,520		
Loan from bank	36,000		
Discounts allowed	7,680		
Discounts received	4,680		
Rent expense	16,080		
Totals			

Task 11.3

The double-entry system of bookkeeping normally results in which of the following balances on the ledger accounts?

Debit balances	Credit balances	✓
Assets and income	Liabilities, capital and expenses	
Income, capital and liabilities	Assets and expenses	
Assets and expenses	Liabilities, capital and income	
Assets, expenses and capital	Liabilities and income	

Task 11.4

A credit balance on a ledger account indicates

	✓
An asset or an expense	
A liability or an expense	
An amount owing to the organisation	
A liability or income	

Task 11.5

Which of the following balances would be a credit balance on a trial balance?

	✓
Non-current assets	
Sales returns	
Discounts allowed	
Bank overdraft	

Task 11.6

Given below is the list of ledger balances for your organisation at 31 August.

You are required to prepare a trial balance as at 31 August.

	£	Debit £	Credit £
Bank (overdraft)	4,838		
Capital	216,000		
Discounts allowed	18,432		
Discounts received	11,232		
Drawings	28,896		
Electricity	8,064		
Loan from bank	86,400		
Motor vehicles	184,320		
Office equipment	87,456		
Petty cash	100		
Purchases	472,320		
Purchases ledger control	86,688		
Purchases returns	10,368		
Rent expense	38,592		
Sales	685,440		
Sales ledger control	103,104		
Sales returns	13,536		
Telephone	4,608		
VAT (owed to HMRC)	37,310		
Wages	178,848		
Totals			

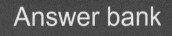

Answer bank

Answer bank

Processing Bookkeeping Transactions Answer bank

Chapter 1

Task 1.1

	Cash transaction ✓	Credit transaction ✓
Purchase of goods for £200 payable by cash in one week's time		✓
Writing a cheque for the purchase of a new computer	✓	
Sale of goods to a customer where the invoice accompanies the goods		✓
Receipt of a cheque from a customer for goods purchased today	✓	
Purchase of goods where payment is due in three weeks' time		✓

Task 1.2

The correct answer is: an invoice

Task 1.3

The correct answer is: an alpha-numeric system

Chapter 2

Task 2.1

The correct answer is: a trade discount

Task 2.2

The correct answer is: HM Revenue & Customs

Task 2.3

Goods total	Trade discount (15% × price) £	Net total £
£416.80	62.52	354.28
£105.60	15.84	89.76
£96.40	14.46	81.94
£263.20	39.48	223.72
£351.00	52.65	298.35

Task 2.4

Net total	VAT (Net × 20%) £	Gross total £
£258.90	51.78	310.68
£316.80	63.36	380.16
£82.60	16.52	99.12
£152.70	30.54	183.24
£451.30	90.26	541.56

Task 2.5

Net total	VAT (Note) £	Gross total £
£258.90	50.22	309.12
£316.80	61.45	378.25
£82.60	16.02	98.62
£152.70	29.62	182.32
£451.30	87.55	538.85

Note: The VAT is calculated on the net total **after** deducting the settlement discount:

(Net total – (Net total × 3%)) × 20/100. The VAT amount is always rounded **down** to the nearest penny.

Task 2.6

Gross total £	VAT (Invoice total × 20/120) £	Net total £
145.20	24.20	121.00
66.90	11.15	55.75
246.60	41.10	205.50
35.40	5.90	29.50
125.40	20.90	104.50

Task 2.7

Invoice total £	VAT (Invoice total × 20/120) £	Net total £
252.66	42.11	210.55
169.20	28.20	141.00
48.60	8.10	40.50
104.28	17.38	86.90
60.48	10.08	50.40
822.60	137.10	685.50

Chapter 3

Task 3.1

The correct answer is £120 (100 + (100 × 20/100) = 120)

Task 3.2

The correct answer is £108 ((100 – (100 × 10/100)) = 90 + (90 × 20/100) = 108)

Task 3.3

(a) – (b) Sales day book

Customer	Invoice number	Total £	VAT £	Net £
Hoppers Ltd	6237	656.40	109.40	547.00
Body Perfect	6238	744.00	124.00	620.00
Esporta Leisure	6239	415.20	69.20	346.00
Langans Beauty	6240	273.60	45.60	228.00
Body Perfect	6241	657.60	109.60	548.00
Superior Products	6242	265.20	44.20	221.00
Esporta Leisure	6243	499.20	83.20	416.00
Hoppers Ltd	6244	285.60	47.60	238.00
Langans Beauty	6245	328.80	54.80	274.00
		4,125.60	687.60	3,438.00

Cross-cast check:

	£
Net	3,438.00
VAT	687.60
Total	4,125.60

Task 3.4

Sales returns day book

Customer	Credit note number	Total £	VAT £	Net £
Hoppers Ltd	1476	82.44	13.74	68.70
Esporta Leisure	1477	107.04	17.84	89.20
Superior Products	1478	14.10	2.35	11.75
		203.58	33.93	169.65

Cross-cast check:

	£
Net	169.65
VAT	33.93
Total	203.58

Task 3.5

(a) – (b) Purchases day book

Date	Supplier	Invoice number	Total £	VAT £	Purchases (materials) £	Stationery £	Packaging £
4 Jan	P J Phillips	03576	428.40	71.40	357.00		
6 Jan	Trenter Ltd	18435	513.60	85.60	428.00		
9 Jan	W J Jones	43654	252.00	42.00		210.00	
12 Jan	P J Phillips	03598	495.60	82.60	413.00		
16 Jan	Packing Supplies	28423	321.60	53.60			268.00
19 Jan	Trenter Ltd	18478	625.20	104.20	521.00		
20 Jan	O & P Ltd	84335	748.80	124.80	624.00		
24 Jan	Packing Supplies	28444	196.80	32.80			164.00
28 Jan	Trenter Ltd	18491	441.60	73.60	368.00		
31 Jan	W J Jones	43681	124.80	20.80		104.00	
			4,148.40	691.40	2,711.00	314.00	432.00

Cross-cast check:

	£
Packaging	432.00
Stationery	314.00
Purchases (materials)	2,711.00
VAT	691.40
Total	4,148.40

Task 3.6

Purchases returns day book

Date	Supplier	Credit note number	Total £	VAT £	Purchases (materials) £	Stationery £	Packaging £
10 Jan	P J Phillips	04216	117.60	19.60	98.00		
16 Jan	W J Jones	0643	67.20	11.20		56.00	
30 Jan	O & P Ltd	1102	148.80	24.80	124.00		
			333.60	55.60	222.00	56.00	

Cross-cast check:

	£
Packaging	0.00
Stationery	56.00
Purchases (materials)	222.00
VAT	55.60
Total	333.60

Chapter 4

Task 4.1

The correct answer is: a price list

Task 4.2

The correct answer is: allocate one of two sales codes to each invoice and use this to write up the invoices in the analysed sales day book

Task 4.3

INVOICE number	57104		
Southfield Electrical, Industrial Estate, Benham DR6 2FF			
VAT registration:	0264 2274 49		
Date/tax point:	8/1/XX		
Order number:	32431		
Customer:	Whitehill Superstores		
Account number (customer code)	SL 44		
Product code	**Quantity**	**Unit amount £**	**Total £**
6060	8	300.00	2,400.00
Trade discount 10	%		240.00
Net total			2,160.00
VAT at 20%			414.72
Total			2,574.72
Settlement discount		4	%

INVOICE number		57105		
Southfield Electrical, Industrial Estate, Benham DR6 2FF				
VAT registration:		0264 2274 49		
Date/tax point:		8/1/XX		
Order number:		24316		
Customer name:		Quinn Ltd		
Account number (customer code)		SL 04		
Product code		Quantity	Unit amount £	Total £
3170		14	35.00	490.00
Trade discount	15	%		73.50
Net total				416.50
VAT at 20%				83.30
Total				499.80
Settlement discount			0	%

INVOICE number		57106		
Southfield Electrical, Industrial Estate, Benham DR6 2FF				
VAT registration:		0264 2274 49		
Date/tax point:		8/1/XX		
Order number:		04367		
Customer:		Harper & Sons		
Account number (customer code)		SL 26		
Product code		Quantity	Unit amount £	Total £
6150		3	260.00	780.00
Trade discount	10	%		78.00
Net total				702.00
VAT at 20%				136.18
Total				838.18
Settlement discount			3	%

Task 4.4

The invoice is for 15 toasters (as ordered) whereas the delivery note shows that only 12 were delivered – the invoice should be amended to show only 12 toasters and the reason for the short delivery should be investigated.

The invoice is charging the vacuums at £220 each whereas the purchase order shows a unit price of £210 – this difference should be investigated – was it agreed in a price quotation to Whitehill that the price would be only £210?

Task 4.5

Errors on the credit note:

- The calculation of the total for the whisks is incorrect.
- The trade discount has been omitted.
- The VAT has been rounded up (not down) and has been deducted rather than added.

Corrected figures:

	£
Fridges	660.00
Whisks (2 × £6.99)	13.98
	673.98
Less 20% trade discount (rounded up to nearest penny)	(134.80)
Net total	539.18
VAT (rounded down to nearest penny)	107.83
Gross total	647.01

Task 4.6

(a) – (b)

Date	Customer	Credit note number	Customer code	Gross total £	VAT £	Net £
21/9	Whitehill Superstores	08650	SL 44	356.40	59.40	297.00
23/9	Dagwell Enterprises	08651	SL 15	244.80	40.80	204.00
	Totals			601.20	100.20	501.00

Task 4.7

Sales ledger

Alpha Services — SL 10

Details	£	Details	£
Balance b/d	253.63	SRDB – 551	624.00
SDB – 715	5,190.00	CB – 013278	253.63
SDB – 787	10,020.00		

STATEMENT OF ACCOUNT	
Southfield Electrical	
Industrial Estate	
Benham DR6 2FF	
Tel: 01239 345639	
VAT registration:	0264 2274 49
Date:	31 May 20XX
Customer:	Alpha Services 83 Abbey Road Durringham DU5 2WP
Account number (customer code)	SL 10

Date	Details	Debit £	Credit £	Balance £
1/5/XX	Bal b/d			253.63
2/5/XX Payment received – thank you			253.63	0.00
7/5/XX	Inv 715	5,190.00		5,190.00
12/5/XX	CN 551		624.00	4,566.00
17/5/XX	Inv 787	10,020.00		14,586.00
Amount now due				14,586.00

Task 4.8

Cheque from Hayworth Ltd for £516.09 – a settlement discount of £448.00 × 4% = £17.92 has been deducted: £534.01 – £17.92 = £516.09. This should not have been taken as the cheque arrived 13 days after the invoice date.

Cheque from Harper & Sons for £709.48 – a discount of £29.56 has been taken. Taking a 4% discount is valid but it has been incorrectly calculated. The correct discount is £620.00 × 4/100 = £24.80. Therefore the cheque should have been made out for £739.04 – £24.80 = £714.24.

Chapter 5

Task 5.1

When a supplier delivers materials to him he retains the supplier's delivery note and also prepares | **a goods received note** | once he has had a chance to inspect the quality of the items.

Task 5.2

The correct answer is: a product code

Task 5.3

(a) The correct answer is: 20 June

(b) The correct answer is: £235.20

Workings

Discount: (239.20 – 39.20) × 2/100 = 4.00

Payment: 239.2 – 4.00 = 235.20

Task 5.4

Invoice date	Supplier name	Payment date	Working	Amount of cheque £
5 Jan	Henson Press	27 Jan		336.00
8 Jan	GH Publications	3 Feb		136.80
12 Jan	Ely Instruments	27 Jan	£640.00 – (2% × 640.00) + 125.44	752.64
15 Jan	Hams Instruments	10 Feb		370.45
19 Jan	CD Supplies	10 Feb		138.02
22 Jan	Jester Press	27 Jan	£127.60 – (3.5% × 127.60) + 24.62	147.75
22 Jan	Henson Press	17 Feb		306.00
23 Jan	CD Supplies	27 Jan	£65.40 – (3% × 65.40) + 12.68	76.12
25 Jan	Jester Press	27 Jan	£39.50 – (3.5% × 39.50) + 7.62	45.74
25 Jan	Buser Ltd	27 Jan	£245.00 – (5% × 245.00) + 46.55	279.30

Task 5.5

REMITTANCE ADVICE

To: P.T. Supplies
28 Farm Court Road
Drenchley DR22 4XT

From: Edgehill Designs

Date: 7 February 20XX

Reference	Amount £	Paid (✓)
20671	107.22	✓
20692	157.63	✓
CN 04722	(28.41)	✓

CHEQUE ENCLOSED	£236.44

Task 5.6

- The invoice quantity agrees to the purchase order but the delivery note and GRN show that only 6 tumble dryers were delivered.

- The calculation of the total cost of the tumble dryers is incorrect. It should be £1,715 (7 × £245) not £1,778.

- The VAT calculation is incorrect – it should be:

	£
Net total	1,821.42
Less settlement discount (£1,821.42 × 4/100)	(72.86)
	1,748.56
VAT £1,748.56 × 20/100 (rounded down)	349.71

BPP
LEARNING MEDIA

Task 5.7

- No trade discount has been deducted despite the supplier's file showing that a trade discount of 10% is normally deducted.

- The net total of the goods is incorrect and should total £2,508, not £2,535.

Task 5.8

Purchases day book

Date 20XX	Details	Invoice number	Total £	VAT £	Net £
30 June	Seashell Ltd	8971	3,788.98	577.98	3,211.00
30 June	Opal & Co	05119	4,800.00	800.00	4,000.00
	Totals		8,588.98	1,377.98	7,211.00

Purchases ledger

Account name	Amount £	Debit ✓	Credit ✓
Seashell Ltd	3,788.98		✓
Opal & Co	4,800.00		✓

Task 5.9

(a) The correct answer is: discount received £20

(b) The correct answer is: credit note 3215 £250

(c) The correct answer is: £723

Working

£743 − £20 = £723

Task 5.10

VAT: ((30 × 20) – (30 × 20 × 10/100)) × 20/100

Total: (30 × 20) – (30 × 20 × 10/100) + 108.00

	Yes ✓	No ✓
Has the correct purchase price of the cardboard boxes been charged?		✓
Has the correct discount been applied?		✓
What would be the VAT amount charged if the invoice was correct?	£	108.00
What would be the total amount charged if the invoice was correct?	£	648.00

Task 5.11

(a)

Ken's Exotics
1 Bath Street
Cembury, CE11 9SD

REMITTANCE ADVICE

To: Mack Materials   Date: 30 June 20XX

Please find attached our cheque in payment of the following amounts.

Invoice number	Credit note number	Amount £
901		760
	43	31
Total amount paid		729

(b) The correct answer is: the remittance advice note will be sent to the supplier to advise them of the amount being paid

Task 5.12

The correct answer is: Ken sent a cheque for £1,586 to the supplier on 30 June 20XX

Chapter 6

Task 6.1

	Asset ✓	Liability ✓
A trade receivable	✓	
A car used in the business	✓	
A loan from the bank		✓
A bank overdraft		✓
Cash in hand	✓	
VAT owed to HMRC		✓
A trade payable		✓
Inventory of raw materials	✓	

Task 6.2

An increase in an expense is a | debit |
A decrease in a liability is a | debit |
An increase in income is a | credit |
An increase in an asset is a | debit |
An increase in capital is a | credit |
A decrease in an asset is a | credit |
An increase in a liability is a | credit |
A decrease in capital is a | debit |

Task 6.3

(i)   James paid £20,000 into a business bank account in order to start the business.

Effect 1	Effect 2
Increase in cash	Increase in capital of business on set-up

(ii)   He paid an initial rental of £2,500 by cheque for the shop that he is to trade from.

Effect 1	Effect 2
Decrease in cash	Rent expense incurred

(iii) He purchased a van by cheque for £7,400.

Effect 1	Effect 2
Decrease in cash	Increase in asset – the van

(iv) He purchased £6,000 of goods for resale on credit.

Effect 1	Effect 2
Increase in purchases	Increase in trade payables

(v)   He sold goods for £1,000 - the customer paid by cheque.

Effect 1	Effect 2
Increase in cash	Increase in sales

(vi) He sold goods on credit for £4,800.

Effect 1	Effect 2
Increase in trade receivables	Increase in sales

(vii) He paid shop assistants' wages by cheque totalling £2,100.

Effect 1	Effect 2
Decrease in cash	Wages expense incurred

(viii) He made further sales on credit for £3,900.

Effect 1	Effect 2
Increase in trade receivables	Increase in sales

(ix) He purchased a further £1,400 of goods for resale by cheque.

Effect 1	Effect 2
Decrease in cash	Increase in purchases

(x)   £3,700 was received from credit customers.

Effect 1	Effect 2
Increase in cash	Decrease in trade receivables

(xi) He paid £3,300 to credit suppliers.

Effect 1	Effect 2
Decrease in cash	Decrease in trade payables

(xii) He withdrew £800 from the business for his living expenses.

Effect 1	Effect 2
Decrease in cash	Increase in drawings

Task 6.4

Bank

Details	£	Details	£
Capital (i)	20,000	Rent (ii)	2,500
Sales (v)	1,000	Van (iii)	7,400
Sales ledger control (x)	3,700	Wages (vii)	2,100
		Purchases (ix)	1,400
		Purchases ledger control (xi)	3,300
		Drawings (xii)	800

Capital

Details	£	Details	£
		Bank (i)	20,000

Rent

Details	£	Details	£
Bank (ii)	2,500		

Van

Details	£	Details	£
Bank (iii)	7,400		

Purchases

Details	£	Details	£
Purchases ledger control (iv)	6,000		
Bank (ix)	1,400		

Purchases ledger control

Details	£	Details	£
Bank (xi)	3,300	Purchases (iv)	6,000

Sales account

Details	£	Details	£
		Bank (v)	1,000
		Sales ledger control (vi)	4,800
		Sales ledger control (viii)	3,900

Sales ledger control

Details	£	Details	£
Sales (vi)	4,800	Bank (x)	3,700
Sales (viii)	3,900		

Wages

Details	£	Details	£
Bank (vii)	2,100		

Drawings

Details	£	Details	£
Bank (xii)	800		

Task 6.5

	Debit ✓	Credit ✓
Discounts allowed	✓	
Sales ledger control		✓

Task 6.6

T N Designs

	£		£
1 May balance b/d	2,643.56	8 May CB	1,473.28
11 May SDB – 27491	828.40	24 May SRDB Cn0381	256.89
18 May SDB – 27513	1,088.65	31 May balance c/d	2,830.44
	4,560.61		4,560.61

Harold & Partners

	£		£
1 May balance b/d	1,367.83	7 MAY CB	635.78
5 May SDB – 27465	998.20	7 May CB – discount	33.46
12 May SDB – 27499	478.92	15 May SRDB – Cn0364	106.34
20 May SDB – 27524	258.28	30 May CB	663.66
		30 May CB – discount	34.93
		31 May balance c/d	1,629.06
	3,103.23		3,103.24

Task 6.7

	Debit £	Credit £
Purchases ledger control	367.48	
Bank		367.48
Purchases ledger control	12.50	
Discount received		12.50

Task 6.8

	Capital ✓	Revenue ✓
Purchase of a new computer paid for by cheque	✓	
Purchase of printer paper by cheque		✓
Purchase of a new business car on credit	✓	
Payment of road tax on a new business car		✓
Payment of rent for the business premises		✓

Task 6.9

Purchases ledger control

Date	Details	£	Date	Details	£
31 Oct	Purchases returns	4,467	1 Oct	Balance b/d	41,204
31 Oct	Bank	36,409	31 Oct	Purchases	52,390
31 Oct	Discounts received	125			
31 Oct	Balance c/d	52,593			
		93,594			93,594
			1 Nov	Balance b/d	52,593

Petty cash

Date	Details	£	Date	Details	£
1 Oct	Balance b/d	200.00	31 Oct	Expenses	183.25
31 Oct	Bank	183.25	31 Oct	Balance c/d	200.00
		383.25			383.25
1 Nov	Balance b/d	200.00			

VAT

Date	Details	£	Date	Details	£
31 Oct	Sales returns	40.00	1 Oct	Balance b/d	183.25
31 Oct	Purchases	1,900.00	31 Oct	Purchases returns	62.00
31 Oct	Balance c/d	1,555.25	31 Oct	Sales	3,250.00
		3,495.25			3,495.25
			1 Nov	Balance b/d	1,555.25

Task 6.10

	Capital ✓	Revenue ✓
Payment of a credit supplier for goods received for resale		✓
Receipt of proceeds from sale of car used in the business	✓	
Payment of drawings to the business owner	✓	
Acquisition of new machine for use over five years	✓	
Payment by a cash customer for goods		✓

Chapter 7

Task 7.1

(a) – (b)

Date	Details	Cheque No	Discounts received £	Cash £	Bank £	VAT £	Cash purchases £	Trade payables £
10 Jul	W J Jones	002156	10.50		521.36			521.36
10 Jul	Cash purchase			415.80		69.30	346.50	
11 Jul	Trenter Ltd	002157			358.65			358.65
11 Jul	Packing Supp	002158	26.30		754.36			754.36
11 Jul	Cash purchase			85.80		14.30	71.50	
12 Jul	P J Phillips	002159			231.98			231.98
13 Jul	O & P Ltd	002160	17.56		721.30			721.30
14 Jul	Cash purchase			107.52		17.92	89.60	
			54.36	609.12	2,587.65	101.52	507.60	2,587.65

Cross-cast check:

	£
Trade payables	2,587.65
Cash purchases	507.60
VAT	101.52
Total	3,196.77
Cash	609.12
Bank	2,587.65
Total	3,196.77

Task 7.2

Cash book – credit side

Date	Details	Cheque No	Discounts received £	Cash £	Bank £	VAT £	Trade payables £	Rent & rates £
27 Jan	Henson Press	003014			329.00		329.00	
27 Jan	Ely	003015	12.80		736.96		736.96	
27 Jan	Jester Press	003016	4.47		144.67		144.67	
27 Jan	CD Supplies	003017	1.96		74.54		74.54	
27 Jan	Jester Press	003018	1.38		44.79		44.79	
27 Jan	Buser Ltd	003019	12.25		273.48		273.48	
27 Jan	Rates	SO			255.00			255.00
27 Jan	Rent	DD			500.00			500.00
			32.86		2,358.44		1,603.44	755.00

Cross-cast check:

	£
Rent & rates	755.00
Trade payables	1,603.44
Total	2,358.44
Cash	0.00
Bank	2,358.44
Total	2,358.44

Task 7.3

(a) – (b)

Cash book

Date	Details	Discounts allowed £	Cash £	Bank £	VAT £	Cash sales £	Trade receivables £
10 Jul	Superior Products	32.56		891.36			891.36
11 Jul	Hoppers Ltd			295.68			295.68
11 Jul	Cash sales		138.24		23.04	115.20	
13 Jul	Body Perfect	21.45		542.97			542.97
13 Jul	Cash sales		209.76		34.96	174.80	
14 Jul	Esporta Leisure	42.58		958.45			958.45
14 Jul	Cash sales		84.48		14.08	70.40	
14 Jul	Langans Beauty			752.45			752.45
		96.59	432.48	3,440.91	72.08	360.40	3,440.91

Cross-cast check:

	£
Trade receivables	3,440.91
Cash sales	360.40
VAT	72.08
Total	3,873.39
Cash	432.48
Bank	3,440.91
Total	3,873.39

Task 7.4

(a) **Cash book – credit side**

Details	Discounts £	Cash £	Bank £	VAT £	Trade payables £	Cash purchases £	Stationery £
Balance b/f			236				
Dubai Dreams		324		54		270	
Walter Enterprises		228		38		190	
Sinead Reilly		56				56	
Sumatra Trading	35		7,265		7,265		
SHSK Co			378	63			315
Total	35	608	7,879	155	7,265	516	315

(b)

Details	Discounts £	Cash £	Bank £	Trade receivables £
Balance b/f		1,228		
Park Farm Stores			2,576	2,576
Tristram Pale Ltd	25		4,233	4,233
Total	25	1,228	6,809	6,809

(c) The correct answer is: £620

Working

(1,228 – 608)

(d) The correct answer is: £1,070

Working

(7,879 – 6,809)

(e) The correct answer is: Credit

Task 7.5

(a) **Cash book – credit side**

Details	Discount £	Cash £	Bank £	VAT £	Trade payables £	Cash purchases £	Motor expenses £
Balance b/f			16,942				
B Smithson Ltd		240		40		200	
H Hamnet		192		32		160	
Renee Reid		320				320	
Tenon Ltd	80		3,600		3,600		
Vernon Motor Repairs			48	8			40
Total	80	752	20,590	80	3,600	680	40

(b) **Cash book – debit side**

Details	Discount £	Cash £	Bank £	Trade receivables £
Balance b/f		1,325		
G Brownlow			749	749
S Barnett	30		300	300
Total	30	1,325	1,049	1,049

(c) The correct answer is: £573

Working

(1,325 – 752 = 573)

(d) The correct answer is: £19,541

Working

(20,590 – 1,049 = 19,541)

(e) The correct answer is: Credit

Chapter 8

Task 8.1

Sales day book

Date 20XX	Customer	Invoice number	Customer code	Total £	VAT (Total × 20/120) £	Net £
Jan	H Simms	0001	SL 45	1,800	300	1,500
Jan	P Good	0002	SL 21	3,000	500	2,500
Jan	K Mitchell	0003	SL 30	912	152	760
Jan	C Brown	0004	SL 05	2,790	465	2,325
Totals				8,502	1,417	7,085

Cash book – debit side

Date 20XX	Details	Bank £	VAT £	Cash sales £	Trade receivables £
Jan	From H Simms	900.00			900.00
Jan	From P Good	1,400.00			1,400.00
Jan	From K Mitchell	912.00			912.00
Jan	From C Brown	490.00			490.00
Totals		3,702.00			3,702.00

General ledger

Sales ledger control

Details	£	Details	£
Sales	8,502.00	Bank	3,702.00

Sales

Details	£	Details	£
		SLCA	7,085.00

VAT

Details	£	Details	£
		Sales	1,417.00

Sales ledger

H Simms SL 45

Details	£	Details	£
SDB 0001	1,800.00	CB	900.00

P Good SL 21

Details	£	Details	£
SDB 0002	3,000.00	CB	1,400.00

K Mitchell SL 30

Details	£	Details	£
SDB 0003	912.00	CB	912.00

C Brown SL 05

Details	£	Details	£
SDB 0004	2,790.00	CB	490.00

Task 8.2

(a) General ledger

Sales ledger control

Details	£	Details	£
Sales	4,125.60		

VAT

Details	£	Details	£
		Sales	687.60

Sales

Details	£	Details	£
		SLCA	3,438.00

(b) Sales ledger

Hoppers Ltd

Details	£	Details	£
SDB 6237	656.40		
SDB 6244	285.60		

Body Perfect

Details	£	Details	£
SDB 6238	744.00		
SDB 6241	657.60		

Esporta Leisure

Details	£	Details	£
SDB 6239	415.20		
SDB 6243	499.20		

Langans Beauty

Details	£	Details	£
SDB 6240	273.60		
SDB 6245	328.80		

Superior Products

Details	£	Details	£
SDB 6242	265.20		

Task 8.3

(a) Sales day book

Customer	Invoice number	Customer code	Invoice total £	VAT £	Net £
Rocks Garden Suppliers	08663	SL22	701.76	116.96	584.80
Eridge Nurseries	08664	SL07	429.30	71.55	357.75
Abergaven GC	08665	SL16	923.40	153.90	769.50
Rother Nurseries	08666	SL13	756.00	126.00	630.00
			2,810.46	468.41	2,342.05

(b) Cross-cast check:

	£
Net	2,342.05
VAT	468.41
Invoice total	2,810.46

(c) General ledger

Sales ledger control

Details	£	Details	£
Sales	2,810.46		

VAT

Details	£	Details	£
		Sales	468.41

Sales

Details	£	Details	£
		SLCA	2,342.05

Sales ledger

Eridge Nurseries SL 07

Details	£	Details	£
SDB – 08664	429.30		

Rother Nurseries SL 13

Details	£	Details	£
SDB – 08666	756.00		

Abergaven Garden Centre SL 16

Details	£	Details	£
SDB – 08665	923.40		

Rocks Garden Suppliers SL 22

Details	£	Details	£
SDB – 08663	701.76		

Task 8.4

(a) General ledger

Sales ledger control

	£		£
Sales	4,125.60	Sales returns	203.64

VAT

	£		£
Sales returns	33.94	Sales	687.60

Sales returns

	£		£
SLCA	169.70		

(b) **Sales ledger**

Hoppers Ltd

	£		£
SDB – 6237	656.40	SRDB – 1476	82.44
SDB – 6244	285.60		

Body Perfect

	£		£
SDB – 6238	744.00		
SDB – 6241	657.60		

Esporta Leisure

	£		£
SDB – 6239	415.20	SRDB – 1477	107.04
SDB – 6243	499.20		

Langans Beauty

	£		£
SDB – 6240	273.60		
SDB – 6245	328.80		

Superior Products

	£		£
SDB – 6242	265.20	SRDB – 1478	14.16

Task 8.5

	Comments
Payment from Rocks Garden Suppliers	The remittance advice has been wrongly added up – the total should be £879.37
Payment from Eridge Nurseries	This is perfectly acceptable and valid
Payment from Abergaven Garden Centre	This is perfectly acceptable and valid
Payment from Rother Nurseries	On the remittance advice Rother Nurseries has recorded invoice 08674 as £114.78 rather than £214.78 – therefore the amount of the payment is wrong

Task 8.6

General ledger

Cash

Details	£	Details	£
Cash sales	279.84		

Bank

Details	£	Details	£
SLCA	2,018.10		

Sales ledger control

Details	£	Details	£
Sales	4,125.60	Sales returns	203.64
		Bank	2,018.10
		Discounts allowed	53.22

Sales

Details	£	Details	£
		SLCA	3,438.00
		Cash	233.20

VAT

Details	£	Details	£
Sales returns	33.94	Sales	687.60
		Cash	46.64

Discounts allowed

Details	£	Details	£
SLCA	53.22		

Sales ledger

Hoppers Ltd

Details	£	Details	£
SDB – 6237	656.40	SRDB – 1476	82.44
SDB – 6244	285.60	CB	553.96
		CB – discount	20.00

Body Perfect

Details	£		£
SDB – 6238	744.00	CB	706.64
SDB – 6241	657.60	CB – discount	21.86

Esporta Leisure

Details	£	Details	£
SDB – 6239	415.20	SRDB – 1477	107.04
SDB – 6243	499.20	CB	367.20
		CB – discount	11.36

Langans Beauty

Details	£	Details	£
SDB – 6240	273.60	CB	273.60
SDB – 6245	328.80		

Superior Products

Details	£	Details	£
SDB – 6242	265.20	SRDB – 1478	14.16
		CB	116.70

....

Task 8.7

<table>
<tr><td colspan="4" align="center">Ken's Exotics
1 Bath Street
Cembury, CE11 9SD</td></tr>
<tr><td colspan="2">To: Crowley Ltd</td><td colspan="2" align="right">Date: 31 October 20XX</td></tr>
</table>

Date 20XX	Details	Transaction amount £	Outstanding amount £
15/9	Invoice 1540	627	627
29/9	Invoice 1560	728	1,355
3/10	Credit note 89	46	1,309
10/10	Invoice 1580	1,209	2,518
15/10	Cheque	581	1,937

....

Chapter 9

Task 9.1

(a) – (b)

General ledger

Purchases ledger control

Details	£	Details	£
		Purchases etc	4,148.40

VAT

Details	£	Details	£
Purchases etc	691.40		

Purchases

Details	£	Details	£
PLCA	2,711.00		

Stationery

Details	£	Details	£
PLCA	314.00		

Packaging

Details	£	Details	£
PLCA	432.00		

Purchases ledger

P J Phillips

Details	£	Details	£
		PDB 03576	428.40
		PDB 03598	495.60

Trenter Ltd

Details	£	Details	£
		PDB 18435	513.60
		PDB 18478	625.20
		PDB 18491	441.60

O & P Ltd

Details	£	Details	£
		PDB 84335	748.80

W J Jones

Details	£	Details	£
		PDB 43654	252.00
		PDB 43681	124.80

Packing Supplies

Details	£	Details	£
		PDB 28423	321.60
		PDB 28444	196.80

Task 9.2

(a) Purchases day book

Date	Supplier	Invoice number	Supplier code	Total £	VAT £	Net £	Wood purchases £	Polish/ varnish purchases £	Other purchases £
27 Jan	Ephraim Supplies	09642	PL39	349.20	58.20	291.00	291.00		
27 Jan	Cavendish Woods	06932	PL14	846.12	141.02	705.10	705.10		
27 Jan	Calverley Bros	67671	PL03	174.72	29.12	145.60		145.60	
27 Jan	Culverden & Co	36004	PL23	68.88	11.48	57.40			57.40
				1,438.92	239.82	1,199.10	996.10	145.60	57.40

(b) Cross-cast check:

	£
Net	1,199.10
VAT	239.82
Total	1,438.92

(c) General ledger

Purchases ledger control

Details	£		£
		Purchases	1,438.92

VAT

Details	£		£
Purchases	239.82		

Wood purchases

Details	£		£
PLCA	996.10		

Polish/varnish purchases

Details	£		£
PLCA	145.60		

Other purchases

Details	£		£
PLCA	57.40		

(d) **Purchases ledger**

Calverley Bros   **PL 03**

Details	£		£
		PDB 67671	174.72

Cavendish Woods   **PL 14**

Details	£		£
		PDB 06932	846.12

Culverden & Co   **PL 23**

Details	£		£
		PDB 36004	68.88

Ephraim Supplies   **PL 39**

Details	£		£
		PDB 09642	349.20

Task 9.3

(a) **General ledger**

Purchases ledger control

Details	£	Details	£
Purchases returns	333.60	Purchases etc	4,148.40

VAT

Details	£	Details	£
Purchases etc	691.40	Purchases returns	55.60

Purchases returns

Details	£	Details	£
		PLCA	222.00

Stationery

Details	£	Details	£
PLCA	314.00	PLCA	56.00

(b) **Purchases ledger**

P J Phillips

Details	£	Details	£
PRDB 04216	117.60	PDB 03576	428.40
		PDB 03598	495.60

W J Jones

Details	£	Details	£
PRDB 0643	67.20	PDB 43654	252.00
		PDB 43681	124.80

O & P Ltd

Details	£	Details	£
PRDB 1102	148.80	PDB 84335	748.80

Task 9.4

(a) General ledger

Purchases ledger control

Details	£	Details	£
Purchases returns etc	333.60	Purchases etc	4,148.40
Bank	3,053.37		
Discounts received	35.00		

VAT

Details	£	Details	£
Purchases etc	691.40	Purchases returns etc	55.60
Bank	55.54		

Purchases

Details	£	Details	£
PLCA	2,711.00		
Bank	277.70		

Discounts received

Details	£	Details	£
		PLCA	35.00

(b) Purchases ledger

P J Phillips

Details	£	Details	£
PRDB 04216	117.60	PDB 03576	428.40
CB 002147	806.40	PDB 03598	495.60

Trenter Ltd

Details	£	Details	£
CB 002144	1,105.07	PDB 18435	513.60
CB discount	10.00	PDB 18478	625.20
		PDB 18491	441.60

W J Jones

Details	£	Details	£
PRDB CN0643	67.20	PDB 43654	252.00
CB 002146	252.00	PDB 43681	124.80

O & P Ltd

Details	£	Details	£
PRDB CN1102	148.80	PDB 84335	748.80
CB 002150	580.00		
CB discount	20.00		

Packing Supplies

Details	£	Details	£
CB 002149	309.90	PDB 28423	321.60
CB discount	5.00	PDB 28444	196.80

Task 9.5

(a)

Supplier account code	VIN234
General ledger code	GL505

(b) The correct answer is: to help trace relevant accounts quickly and easily

Chapter 10

Task 10.1

The correct answer is: £68.34

Task 10.2

(a) **Petty cash book**

Debit side			Credit side								
Date	Details	Amount £	Date	Details	Voucher number	Total £	VAT £	Travel £	Post £	Stationery £	Office supplies £
22 Jan	Bal b/f	120.00	23 Jan	Coffee	0721	3.99					3.99
			23 Jan	Stamps	0722	24.00			24.00		
			24 Jan	Taxi fare	0723	10.72	1.78	8.94			
			24 Jan	Paper	0724	7.12	1.18			5.94	
			26 Jan	Train fare	0725	13.60		13.60			
			27 Jan	Disks	0726	11.22	1.87				9.35
						70.65	4.83	22.54	24.00	5.94	13.34

(b) **Cross-cast check:**

	£
Office supplies	13.34
Stationery	5.94
Post	24.00
Travel	22.54
VAT	4.83
Total	70.65

Task 10.3

(a) The correct answer is: £16

Working

	£
Opening balance	22
Cash from bank	53
Less: expenditure during month	(16)
balance at end of month	59

Therefore 75 – 59 = £16 required to restore the imprest level

(b) The correct answer is: Debit

Task 10.4

(a)

	Voucher total
	£
0473	12.60
0474	15.00
0475	19.75
0476	9.65
0477	10.00
0478	13.84
0479	4.26
0480	16.40
	101.50

Petty cash box

		£
£10 note	1	10.00
£5 note	4	20.00
£2 coin	3	6.00
£1 coin	7	7.00
50p coin	5	2.50
20p coin	8	1.60
10p coin	9	0.90
5p coin	4	0.20
2p coin	11	0.22
1p coin	8	0.08
		48.50

	£
Voucher total	101.50
Petty cash in the box	48.50
Imprest amount	150.00

(b)

Petty cash control

		£			£
1 Jan	Balance b/f	150.00	31 Jan	Expenditure	101.50
			31 Jan	Balance c/d	48.50
		150.00			150.00
1 Feb	Balance b/d	48.50			

Task 10.5

(a) – (c)

Date	Details	Amount £	Date	Details	Total £	Stationery £	Postage £	Motor fuel £
1 Nov	Bal b/f	100	7 Nov	Postage stamps	20		20	
			15 Nov	Pens and pencils	18	18		
			22 Nov	Petrol	10			10
			30 Nov	Envelopes	15	15		
					63			
			30 Nov	Bal c/d	37			
	Total	100		Total	100	33	20	10
1 Dec	Bal b/d	37						

Task 10.6

(a) – (b)

Petty cash book

Debit side		Credit side					
Details	Amount £	Details	Amount £	VAT £	Postage £	Travel £	Cleaning £
Balance b/f	175.00	Post Office	30.00		30.00		
		Window cleaning	30.72	5.12			25.60
		MegaBus	29.50			29.50	
		Balance c/d	84.78				
	175.00		175.00	5.12	30.00	29.50	25.60

Task 10.7

(a)

Amount in petty cash box	£	91.70
Balance on petty cash control account	£	96.70
Difference	£	5.00

(b)

Petty cash reimbursement		
Date: 30.09.20XX		
Amount required to restore the cash in the petty cash box	£	240.24

Task 10.8

(a) – (b)

Petty cash book

Debit side		Credit side					
Details	Amount £	Details	Amount £	VAT £	Postage £	Travel £	Stationery £
Balance b/f	150.00	Tom's Taxi	18.00			18.00	
		Post Office	30.00		30.00		
		SMP Stationery	43.20	7.20			36.00
		Balance c/d	58.80				
	150.00		150.00	7.20	30.00	18.00	36.00

Task 10.9

(a)

Amount in petty cash box	£	116.15
Balance on petty cash control account	£	120.00
Difference	£	3.85

(b)

Petty cash reimbursement		
Date: 31.07.20XX		
Amount required to restore the cash in the petty cash box	£	196.55

Task 10.10

(a)

General ledger

Account name	Amount £	Debit ✓	Credit ✓
Petty cash	108.32		✓
VAT	15.52	✓	
Office expenses	15.20	✓	
Stationery	32.60	✓	
Maintenance	45.00	✓	

(b) The credit entry to petty cash would not be needed if the petty cash book was itself part of the general ledger double entry system.

Chapter 11

Task 11.1

Ledger account	Balance	Debit ✓	Credit ✓
Sales	592,513		✓
Telephone	1,295	✓	
Sales ledger control	52,375	✓	
Wages	104,288	✓	
Purchases returns	8,229		✓
Bank overdraft	17,339		✓
Purchases	372,589	✓	
Drawings	71,604	✓	
Sales returns	32,800	✓	
Car	14,700	✓	
Purchases ledger control	31,570		✓

Task 11.2

	£	Debit £	Credit £
Motor vehicles	76,800	76,800	
Office equipment	36,440	36,440	
Sales	285,600		285,600
Purchases	196,800	196,800	
Bank (overdraft)	2,016		2,016
Petty cash	36	36	
Capital	90,000		90,000
Sales returns	5,640	5,640	
Purchases returns	4,320		4,320
Sales ledger control	42,960	42,960	
Purchases ledger control	36,120		36,120
VAT (owed to HMRC)	15,540		15,540
Drawings	12,040	12,040	
Telephone	1,920	1,920	
Electricity	3,360	3,360	
Wages	74,520	74,520	
Loan from bank	36,000		36,000
Discounts allowed	7,680	7,680	
Discounts received	4,680		4,680
Rent expense	16,080	16,080	
Totals		474,276	474,276

Task 11.3

Debit balances	Credit balances	
Assets and expenses	Liabilities, capital and income	✓

Task 11.4

The correct answer is: a liability or income

Task 11.5

The correct answer is: bank overdraft

··

Task 11.6

	£	Debit £	Credit £
Bank (overdraft)	4,838		4,838
Capital	216,000		216,000
Discounts allowed	18,432	18,432	
Discounts received	11,232		11,232
Drawings	28,896	28,896	
Electricity	8,064	8,064	
Loan from bank	86,400		86,400
Motor vehicles	184,320	184,320	
Office equipment	87,456	87,456	
Petty cash	100	100	
Purchases	472,320	472,320	
Purchases ledger control	86,688		86,688
Purchases returns	10,368		10,368
Rent expense	38,592	38,592	
Sales	685,440		685,440
Sales ledger control	103,104	103,104	
Sales returns	13,536	13,536	
Telephone	4,608	4,608	
VAT (owed to HMRC)	37,310		37,310
Wages	178,848	178,848	
Totals		1,138,276	1,138,276

··

Answer bank

AAT AQ2013 SAMPLE ASSESSMENT 1
PROCESSING BOOKKEEPING
TRANSACTIONS

Time allowed: 2 hours

AAT AQ2013
SAMPLE ASSESSMENT 1

Task 1 (15 marks)

Purchase invoices and purchase credit notes have been received and partially entered in the day-books, as shown below.

Complete the entries in the purchases day-book and the purchases returns day-book by:

(a) **Selecting the correct supplier account codes from the coding list below.**

(b) **Inserting the appropriate figures to complete the entries.**

Coding list

Supplier name	Supplier account code
Cox and Co	COX001
GBL Ltd	GBL001
R King	KIN001
JAB Ltd	JAB001
Jackson plc	JAC002
Johnson Ltd	JOH003
PDL Designs	PDL001
K Ponti	PON002
Proctor Ltd	PRO003

Purchases day-book

Date 20XX	Details	Supplier account code	Invoice number	Total £	VAT £	Net £	Product A100 £	Product B100 £
30 Jun	GBL Ltd	▼	G1161	348		290		290
30 Jun	Jackson plc	▼	4041		125		625	
30 Jun	R King	▼	J1126	612			275	235

Drop-down list:

COX001
GBL001
KIN001
JAB001
JAC002
JOH003
PDL001
PON002
PRO003

Purchases returns day-book

Date 20XX	Details	Supplier account code	Credit note number	Total £	VAT £	Net £	Product A100 £	Product B100 £
30 Jun	PDL Designs	▼	CN110				560	200
30 Jun	K Ponti	▼	398C		95		225	250

Drop-down list:

COX001
GBL001
KIN001
JAB001
JAC002
JOH003
PDL001
PON002
PRO003

Task 2 (15 marks)

The following credit transactions have been entered into the sales returns day-book as shown below. No entries have yet been made into the ledgers.

Sales returns day-book

Date 20XX	Details	Credit note number	Total £	VAT £	Net £
30 Jun	Wem Designs	CN221	1,128	188	940
30 Jun	Bailey and Byng	CN222	354	59	295
	Totals		1,482	247	1,235

(a) **What will be the entries in the sales ledger?**

Sales ledger

Account name	Amount £	Debit	Credit
▼			
▼			

Drop-down list:

Bailey and Byng
Purchases
Purchases ledger control
Purchases returns
Sales
Sales ledger control
Sales returns
VAT
Wem Designs

(b) **What will be the entries in the general ledger?**

General ledger

Account name	Amount £	Debit	Credit
▼			
▼			
▼			

Drop-down list:

Bailey and Byng
Purchases
Purchases ledger control
Purchases returns
Sales
Sales ledger control
Sales returns
VAT
Wem Designs

Task 3 (20 marks)

There are three payments to be entered in the credit side of Gold's cash-book during one week.

Cash purchases listing

Suppliers paid in cash	Net £	VAT £	Gross £
Mendip plc	315	63	378

Trade payables listing

Credit suppliers paid by cheque	Amount paid £	Discounts taken £
Landa Ltd	1,950	50
Bebe and Co	726	38

(a) **Enter the details from the cash purchases listing and the trade payables listing into the credit side of the cash-book shown below and total each column.**

Cash book – credit side

Details	Discounts £	Cash £	Bank £	VAT £	Trade payables £	Cash purchases £
Balance b/f			2,312			
▼						
▼						
▼						
Total						

Drop-down list:

Bank
Bebe and Co
Cash
Cash purchases
Discounts
Landa Ltd
Mendip plc
Trade payables
VAT

The debit side of the cash-book shows the cash balance brought forward at the beginning of the week was £200 and a further £319 has been received during the week.

(b) **Using your answer to (a) above, calculate the cash balance.**

£ [   ]

The debit side of the cash-book shows the total amount of money banked during the week was £1,964.

(c) **Using your answer to (a) above, calculate the bank balance. If your calculations show that the bank account is overdrawn, your answer should start with a minus sign, for example –123.**

£ [   ]

Task 4 (15 marks)

Gold's cash-book is both a book of prime entry and part of the double entry bookkeeping system. These are the totals of the columns in the credit site of the cash-book at the end of a month.

Cash-book – credit side

Details	Cash £	Bank £	VAT £	Trade payables £	Cash purchases £	Bank charges £
Totals	1,590	10,948	265	10,900	1,325	48

(a) **What will be the FOUR entries in the general ledger?**

General ledger

Account name	Amount £	Debit	Credit
▼			
▼			
▼			
▼			

Drop-down list:

Bank
Bank charges
Cash
Cash purchases
Cash sales
Details
Purchases ledger control
Sales ledger control
Totals
Trade payables
VAT

One of the bank payments to trade payables was to D B Franks for £264.

(b) **What will be the entry in the purchases ledger?**

Purchases ledger

Account name	Amount £	Debit	Credit
▼			

Drop-down list:

Bank
D B Franks
Gold
Purchases
Purchases ledger
Purchases ledger control
Sales
Sales ledger
Sales ledger control
Trade payables

Task 5 (20 marks)

Gold maintains a petty cash-book as a book of prime entry and part of the double entry bookkeeping system. This is a summary of petty cash transactions in a week.

Train fare paid of £37.05, VAT not applicable.
Envelopes purchased for £20.50, plus VAT.

(a) **Enter the above transactions into the partially completed petty cash-book below.**

(b) **Total the petty cash-book and show the balance carried down.**

Petty cash-book

Details	Amount £	Details	Amount £	VAT £	Travel expenses £	Office expenses £
Balance b/f	120.00	Pens	30.00			30.00
		▼				
		▼				
		▼				
Total	120.00	Totals				

Drop-down list:

Balance b/f
Balance c/d
Envelopes
Office expenses
Train fare
Travel expenses
VAT

(c) **What will be the THREE accounts in the general ledger which will record the above transactions?**

General ledger accounts	
Envelopes	
Office expenses	
Petty cash-book	
Petty cash control	
Train fare	
Travel expenses	
VAT	

At the start of the next week cash was withdrawn from the bank to restore the imprest level of £120.

(d) **What is the amount of cash that would have been withdrawn from the bank to restore the imprest level?**

£ [   ]

These are the notes and coins that are now in the petty cash box.

Notes and coins
4 × £20 notes
5 × £5 notes
11 × £1 coins
4 × 50p coins
8 × 20p coins
8 × 5p coins

(e) **Does the amount of cash in the petty cash box reconcile with the balance in the petty cash-book?**

Yes, the amount of cash in the petty cash box reconciles with the balance in the petty cash-book.	
No, there is not enough cash in the petty cash box.	
No, there is too much cash in the petty cash box.	

Each petty cash claim is accompanied by a petty cash voucher.

(f)   **Select TWO details that should be shown on the petty cash voucher.**

Details	
Name of Managing Director	
Signature of claimant	
Balance of cash in petty cash box	
Balance b/d in petty cash-book	
Amount of cash being claimed	
Amount of imprest level	

Task 6 (20 marks)

Below is the list of balances to be transferred to the trial balance.

Place the figures in the debit or credit column, as appropriate, and total each column. Do not enter figures with decimal places in this task and do not enter a zero in the empty column.

Trial balance as at 30 June

Account name	Amount £	Debit £	Credit £
Miscellaneous expenses	2,116		
Bank interest received	199		
Bank interest paid	342		
Petty cash control	175		
Office expenses	3,793		
Motor expenses	1,118		
Loan from bank	15,000		
Rent and rates	3,000		
Motor vehicles	37,650		
Sales	198,575		
Purchases returns	875		
Sales ledger control	128,331		
Bank (overdraft)	2,246		
Purchases ledger control	55,231		
VAT (owing to HM Revenue & Customs)	4,289		
Wages	37,466		
Purchases	88,172		
Capital	25,748		
Totals			

Task 7 (15 marks)

This is a summary of Judson Ltd's account in Gold's purchases ledger. Judson Ltd has agreed to allow Gold to make payments by the last day of the second month following the month of invoice. For example invoices issued in January will be due for payment by 31 March.

Date 20XX	Details	Amount £
1 April	Invoice J338	1,145
3 April	Invoice J345	1,330
7 May	Invoice J401	2,887
7 May	Credit note C025	1,330
26 May	Credit note C033	236
26 May	Invoice J478	7,216
26 June	Invoice J501	442
30 June	Credit note C040	152

(a) **Complete the table below by:**

- **Inserting the total of transactions with Judson Ltd in each of the months April, May and June.**

- **Showing the dates by which payments should be made by circling the relevant dates.**

Month	Amount £	Payments to be made by
Transactions in April		30 April 31 May 30 June 31 July 31 August
Transactions in May		30 April 31 May 30 June 31 July 31 August
Transactions in June		30 April 31 May 30 June 31 July 31 August

Gold has received the statement of account below from Judson Ltd.

Judson Ltd
26 Winfield Road, Darton, DF15 8RL

To: Gold   STATEMENT OF ACCOUNT

Date 20XX	Invoice/credit note number	Details	Amount £
1 April	J338	Goods	1,145
3 April	J345	Goods	1,330
7 May	C025	Goods returned	1,330
26 May	C033	Goods returned	236
26 May	J478	Goods	7,216
30 June	C040	Goods returned	152
		Total outstanding	7,973

(b) **Using the data in (a) show what TWO items are missing from the statement of account by circling the relevant items.**

Items
Invoice J338   Invoice J345   Invoice J401   Invoice J478   Invoice J501
Credit note C025   Credit note C033   Credit note C040   Cheque

On 10 July Gold received an invoice from Judson Ltd. The invoice is shown below together with the delivery note.

Invoice

```
                Judson Ltd
    26 Winfield Road, Darton, DF15 8RL
      VAT Registration No. 398 3877 00
To: Gold                      10 July 20XX
           Invoice No. J560
                                    £
500 product B226 @ £0.50 each    250.00
VAT @ 20%                          50.00
Total                            300.00

    Terms: 10% discount for payment
             within 10 days.
```

Delivery note

```
                Judson Ltd
    26 Winfield Road, Darton, DF15 8RL
      VAT Registration No. 398 3877 00

       Delivery note DN011988

8 July 20XX

To: Gold Ltd

Please receive 500 product B226.
```

(c) **Check the delivery note and the invoice and answer the following questions.**

Questions	Yes	No
Has the correct net price been calculated?		
Has the correct amount of goods been delivered?		
Has the correct product been delivered?		
Has the correct discount been applied?		

(d) **What will be the correct amounts of the invoice?**

Net amount £	VAT amount £	Gross amount £

Task 8 (15 marks)

Gold has received a cheque for £1,512 from a credit customer, B Cohen, in full settlement of the account. There was no document included with the cheque to show what transactions were included in the payment.

(a) **Show what document the customer should have included with the cheque by circling one document name.**

Document names
Delivery note   Petty cash voucher   Purchase order   Remittance advice note

This is the account of B Cohen in Gold's sales ledger.

B Cohen   **Account code: COH007**

Date 20XX	Details	Amount £	Date 20XX	Details	Amount £
1 Jun	Balance b/f	1,926	3 Jun	Credit note 101	185
25 Jun	Sales invoice 387	314	4 Jun	Bank	1,741
28 Jun	Sales invoice 391	987	21 Jun	Credit note 110	224
29 Jun	Sales invoice 393	1,422			

(b) **Using the drop-down list below, complete the following statement.**

> The cheque from B Cohen for £1,512 has resulted in an [▼]
>
> This probably relates to [▼]
>
> In order to resolve the problem Gold should [▼]
>
> from B Cohen for £ [   ] which will clear the outstanding balance.

Drop-down list:

balance b/f
credit note 110
credit note 101
overpayment
request a credit note
request an invoice
request another cheque
sales invoice 387
sales invoice 391
sales invoice 393
underpayment

On 10 July Gold received the following purchase order from B Cohen. The goods were delivered the following day. The customer has been offered an 8% trade discount and a 2.5% settlement discount for payment within 10 days.

B Cohen
Ravenscourt Road
Darton, DF15 0MX

Purchase Order BCO1157

Gold   10 July 20XX
14 High Street
Darton
DF11 4GX

Please supply 550 units of product code BX26
@ £160.00 per ten, plus VAT.

(c) **Using the drop-down list below, complete the TEN boxes in the sales invoice below.**

Gold
14 High Street, Darton, DF11 4GX

SALES INVOICE 427

Date: [▼]

To: B Cohen   Customer account code: [   ]

        Ravenscourt Road
        Darton, DF 15 OMX   Purchase order no: [   ]

Quantity of units	Product code	Price each £	Total amount after trade discount £	VAT £	Total £

Terms: [▼]

Drop-down list:

10 July 20XX
11 July 20XX
20 July 20XX
21 July 20XX
Net monthly account
30 days net
2.5% settlement discount for payment within 10 days
8% trade discount

Task 9 (15 marks)

The following account is in the sales ledger at the close of day on 30 June.

(a) **Insert the balance carried down together with date and details.**
(b) **Insert the totals.**
(c) **Insert the balance brought down together with date and details.**

J B Mills

Date 20XX	Details	Amount £	Date 20XX	Details	Amount £
1 Jun	Balance b/f	1,585	22 Jun	Bank	678
11 Jun	Invoice 1269	1,804	29 Jun	Credit note 049	607
▼	▼		▼	▼	
	Total			Total	
▼	▼		▼	▼	

Drop-down list:

30 Jun
1 July
Balance b/d
Balance c/d
Gold
J B Mills

(d) **Complete the statement of account to be sent to J B Mills by:**

- **Writing the individual transactions below into the second column of the statement of account**

- **Entering the amount outstanding after every transaction into the final column of the statement of account**

STATEMENT OF ACCOUNT

Gold
14 High Street, Darton, DF11 4GX.

To: J B Mills   Date: 30 June 20XX

Date 20XX	Details of individual transactions	Outstanding amount £
01 June	Opening balance	
11 June		
22 June		
29 June		

Transactions:

Cheque – £678

Credit note 049 – £607

Invoice 1269 – £1,804

Task 10 (15 marks)

Gold started a new business, J Gems, on 1 July with the following assets and liabilities.

Assets and liabilities	£
Motor vehicle	22,615
Loan from bank	10,000
Inventories	9,881
Cash at bank	3,224

(a) **Show the accounting equation on 1 July by inserting the appropriate figures.**

Assets £	Liabilities £	Capital £

On 8 July the new business had the following assets and liabilities.

Assets and liabilities	£
Motor vehicle	22,615
Loan from bank	10,000
Inventories	8,326
Cash at bank	4,922
Trade receivables	7,600
Trade payables	1,270

(b) **Show the accounting equation on 8 July by inserting the appropriate figures.**

Assets £	Liabilities £	Capital £

(c) **Show whether the transactions of J Gems are classified as capital income, revenue income, capital expenditure or revenue expenditure by linking the transactions on the left hand side to the appropriate right hand box.**

Transactions   Income/Expenditure

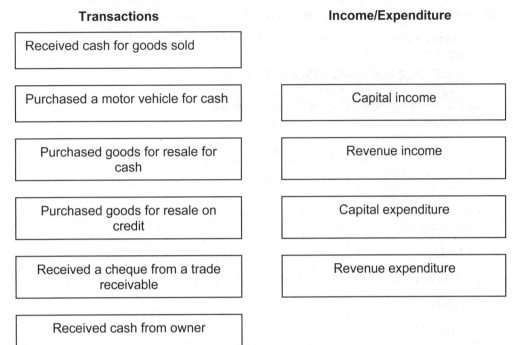

Transactions
Received cash for goods sold
Purchased a motor vehicle for cash
Purchased goods for resale for cash
Purchased goods for resale on credit
Received a cheque from a trade receivable
Received cash from owner

Income/Expenditure
Capital income
Revenue income
Capital expenditure
Revenue expenditure

The goods that J Gems have bought on credit have been entered in the purchases day-book.

(d) **Is the purchases day-book part of the double entry bookkeeping system?**

Yes	
No	

All of J Gems' customers have a customer account code. The codes are made up of the first three letters of the customer's name, followed by the number of the ledger page allocated to each customer in that alphabetical group.

J Gems now has two new customers, MBJ Ltd and Portman and Co.

(e) **Insert the relevant account code in the coding list below for each of the two new customers.**

Customer name	Customer account code
Avion Ltd	AVI01
Blakely plc	BLA01
Brandon and Co	BRA02
Fellows Designs	FEL01
Nailer and Co	NAI01
MBJ Ltd	
Patel Products	PAT01
Pound plc	POU02
Pickford Ltd	PIC03
Portman and Co	
TJK Ltd	TJK01

AAT AQ2013 SAMPLE ASSESSMENT 1 PROCESSING BOOKKEEPING TRANSACTIONS

ANSWERS

Task 1 (15 marks)

(a) – (b)

Purchases day-book

Date 20XX	Details	Supplier account code	Invoice number	Total £	VAT £	Net £	Product A100 £	Product B100 £
30 Jun	GBL Ltd	GBL001	G1161	348	58	290		290
30 Jun	Jackson plc	JAC002	4041	750	125	625	625	
30 Jun	R King	KIN001	J1126	612	102	510	275	235

Purchases returns day-book

Date 20XX	Details	Supplier account code	Credit note number	Total £	VAT £	Net £	Product A100 £	Product B100 £
30 Jun	PDL Designs	PDL001	CN110	912	152	760	560	200
30 Jun	K Ponti	PON002	398C	570	95	475	225	250

Task 2 (15 marks)

(a) **Sales ledger**

Account name	Amount £	Debit	Credit
Wem Designs	1,128		✓
Bailey and Byng	354		✓

(b) **General ledger**

Account name	Amount £	Debit	Credit
Sales returns	1,235	✓	
VAT	247	✓	
Sales ledger control	1,482		✓

Task 3 (20 marks)

(a) **Cash book – credit side**

Details	Discounts £	Cash £	Bank £	VAT £	Trade payables £	Cash purchases £
Balance b/f			2,312			
Mendip plc		378		63		315
Landa Ltd	50		1,950		1,950	
Bebe and Co	38		726		726	
Total	88	378	4,988	63	2,676	315

(b) **Working**: £200 + £319 – £378

£ 141

(c) **Working**: £1,964 – £4,988

– £3,024

Task 4 (15 marks)

(a) **General ledger**

Account name	Amount £	Debit	Credit
VAT	265	✓	
Purchases ledger control account	10,900	✓	
Cash purchases	1,325	✓	
Bank charges	48	✓	

(b) **Purchases ledger**

Account name	Amount £	Debit	Credit
D B Franks	264	✓	

Task 5 (20 marks)

(a) – (b)

Petty cash-book

Tutorial note: The pens would have been subject to VAT if the seller had been VAT-registered, but clearly this was not the case here, and you were not asked to analyse them anyway.

Details	Amount £	Details	Amount £	VAT £	Travel expenses £	Office expenses £
Balance b/f	120.00	Pens	30.00			30.00
		Train fare	37.05		37.05	
		Envelopes	24.60	4.10		20.50
		Balance c/d	28.35			
Total	120.00	Totals	120.00	4.10	37.05	50.50

(c)

General ledger accounts	
Envelopes	
Office expenses	✓
Petty cash-book	
Petty cash control	
Train fare	
Travel expenses	✓
VAT	✓

(d) **Working:** £30.00 + £37.05 + £24.60

£91.65

(e)

Yes, the amount of cash in the petty cash box reconciles with the balance in the petty cash-book.	✓
No, there is not enough cash in the petty cash box.	
No, there is too much cash in the petty cash box.	

(f)

Details	
Name of Managing Director	
Signature of claimant	✓
Balance of cash in petty cash box	
Balance b/d in petty cash-book	
Amount of cash being claimed	✓
Amount of imprest level	

Task 6 (20 marks)

Trial balance as at 30 June

Account name	Amount £	Debit £	Credit £
Miscellaneous expenses	2,116	2,116	
Bank interest received	199		199
Bank interest paid	342	342	
Petty cash control	175	175	
Office expenses	3,793	3,793	
Motor expenses	1,118	1,118	
Loan from bank	15,000		15,000
Rent and rates	3,000	3,000	
Motor vehicles	37,650	37,650	
Sales	198,575		198,575
Purchases returns	875		875
Sales ledger control	128,331	128,331	
Bank (overdraft)	2,246		2,246
Purchases ledger control	55,231		55,231
VAT (owing to HM Revenue & Customs)	4,289		4,289
Wages	37,466	37,466	
Purchases	88,172	88,172	
Capital	25,748		25,748
Totals		302,163	302,163

Task 7 (15 marks)

(a)

Month	Amount £	Payments to be made by
Transactions in April	2,475	30 June
Transactions in May	8,537	31 July
Transactions in June	290	31 August

(b)

Items
Invoice J401   Invoice J501

(c)

Questions	Yes	No
Has the correct net price been calculated?	✓	
Has the correct amount of goods been delivered?	✓	
Has the correct product been delivered?	✓	
Has the correct discount been applied?		✓

(d)

Net amount £	VAT amount £	Gross amount £
250.00	45.00	295.00

Task 8 (15 marks)

(a)

Document names
Remittance advice note

(b)

The cheque from B Cohen for £1,512 has resulted in an **underpayment**.

This probably relates to **sales invoice 391**.

In order to resolve the problem Gold should **request another cheque**

from B Cohen for £**987** which will clear the outstanding balance.

(c)

Gold
14 High Street, Darton, DF11 4GX

SALES INVOICE 427

Date: **11 July 20XX**

To: B Cohen   Customer account code: **COH007**

       Ravenscourt Road
       Darton, DF 15 OMX   Purchase order no: **BCO1157**

Quantity of units	Product code	Price each £	Total amount after trade discount £	VAT £	Total £
550	BX26	16	8,096.00	1,578.72	9,674.72

Terms: 2.5% settlement discount for payment within 10 days

Workings:

$550 \times £16 \times 92\% = £8,096$

$£8,096 \times 97.5\% \times 0.2 = £1,578.72$

Task 9 (15 marks)

(a) – (c)

J B Mills

Date 20XX	Details	Amount £	Date 20XX	Details	Amount £
1 Jun	Balance b/f	1,585	22 Jun	Bank	678
11 Jun	Invoice 1269	1,804	29 Jun	Credit note 049	607
			30 Jun	Balance c/d	2,104
	Total	3,389		Total	3,389
1 Jul	Balance b/d	2,104			

(d)

STATEMENT OF ACCOUNT

Gold
14 High Street, Darton, DF11 4GX.

To: J B Mills   Date: 30 June 20XX

Date 20XX	Details of individual transactions	Outstanding amount £
01 June	Opening balance	1,585
11 June	Invoice 1269 – £1,804	3,389
22 June	Cheque – £678	2,711
29 June	Credit note 049 – £607	2,104

Task 10 (15 marks)

(a)

Assets £	Liabilities £	Capital £
35,720	10,000	25,720

(b)

Assets £	Liabilities £	Capital £
43,463	11,270	32,193

(c)

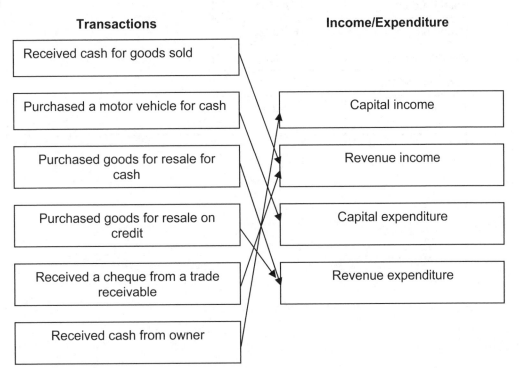

(d) The correct answer is: No

(e)

Customer name	Customer account code
Avion Ltd	AVI01
Blakely plc	BLA01
Brandon and Co	BRA02
Fellows Designs	FEL01
Nailer and Co	NAI01
MBJ Ltd	MBJ01
Patel Products	PAT01
Pound plc	POU02
Pickford Ltd	PIC03
Portman and Co	POR04
TJK Ltd	TJK01

AAT AQ2013 SAMPLE ASSESSMENT 2 PROCESSING BOOKKEEPING TRANSACTIONS

Time allowed: 2 hours

Task 1 (15 marks)

Gold has issued the following sales invoice and sales credit note.

Enter the appropriate details from the sales invoice and the sales credit note into the relevant day-book below.

Gold
14 High Street, Darton, DF11 4GX
VAT Registration No: 298 3837 04
Invoice No. 4789

Date: 30 June 20XX   Customer code: FIR06

To: JJ Firth
        Darton, DF6 7HY

	£
80 items of product AP @ £3.20	256.00
32 items of product AZ @ £5.60	179.20
	435.20
VAT @ 20%	87.04
Total	522.24

Terms: 30 days net

Gold
14 High Street, Darton, DF11 4GX
VAT Registration No: 298 3837 04
Credit Note No. 983

Date: 30 June 20XX   Customer code: COX11

To: Cox plc
        Darton, DF5 6CD

	£
200 items of product AP @ £3.20	640.00
Less 10% bulk discount	64.00
	576.00
VAT @ 20%	115.20
Total	691.20

Terms: 30 days net

Sales day-book

Date 20XX	Details	Customer account code	Invoice number	Total £	VAT £	Net £	Product AP £	Product AZ £
30 Jun	▼							

Drop-down list:

Gold
JJ Firth
Cox plc

Sales returns day-book

Date 20XX	Details	Customer account code	Invoice number	Total £	VAT £	Net £	Product AP £	Product AZ £
30 Jun	▼							

Drop-down list:

Gold
JJ Firth
Cox plc

Task 2 (15 marks)

The following credit transactions have been entered into the purchases returns day-book as shown below. No entries have yet been made into the ledgers.

Purchases returns day-book

Date 20XX	Details	Credit Note Number	Total £	VAT £	Net £
30 Jun	Green and Co	C116	918	153	765
30 Jun	Kitty Cain	CN094	1,344	224	1,120
	Totals		2,262	377	1,885

(a) **What will be the entries in the purchases ledger?**

Purchases ledger

Account name	Amount £	Debit	Credit
▼			
▼			

Drop-down list:

Green and Co
Kitty Cain
Purchases
Purchases ledger control
Purchases returns
Sales
Sales ledger control
Sales returns
VAT

(b) **What will be the entries in the general ledger?**

General ledger

Account name	Amount £	Debit	Credit
▼			
▼			
▼			

Drop-down list:

Green and Co
Kitty Cain
Purchases
Purchases ledger control
Purchases returns
Sales
Sales ledger control
Sales returns
VAT

Task 3 (20 marks)

There are three receipts to be entered in the debit side of Gold's cash-book during one week.

Receipt from a customer who does not have a credit account:

*   Cash received from Bob Sykes of £462 including VAT, for goods sold.

Receipts from credit customers

*   BACS receipts as shown on the remittance advice notes below.

Lynch Ltd

BACS Remittance Advice

To: Gold   1 June 20XX

An amount of £1,988 has been paid directly into your bank account in respect of invoice number G778. A settlement discount of £116 has been taken.

Tara plc

BACS Remittance Advice

To: Gold   1 June 20XX

An amount of £1,219 has been paid directly into your bank account in respect of invoice number G707. A settlement discount of £85 has been taken.

(a) **Enter the details of the three receipts into the debit side of the cash-book shown below and total each column.**

Cash book – debit side

Details	Discounts £	Cash £	Bank £	VAT £	Trade receivables £	Cash sales £
Balance b/f		220				
▼						
▼						
▼						
Total						

Drop-down list:

Bank
Bob Sykes
Cash
Cash sales
Discounts
Lynch Ltd
Tara plc
Trade receivables
VAT

The credit side of the cash-book shows total cash payments during the week were £489.

(b) Using your answer to (a) above, calculate the cash balance.

£ _____

The credit side of the cash-book shows the bank balance brought forward at the beginning of the week was £1,146 overdrawn and total bank payments during the week were £2,907.

(c) Using your answer to (a) above, calculate the bank balance. If your calculations show that the bank account is overdrawn, your answer should start with a minus sign, for example –123.

£ _____

Task 4 (15 marks)

Gold's cash-book Is a book of prime entry only and not part of the double entry bookkeeping system. There was no opening bank balance at the start of the month. These are the totals of the columns in the debit side of the cash-book at the end of the month.

Cash-book – debit side

Details	Cash £	Bank £	VAT £	Trade receivables £	Cash sales £	Rent received £
Totals	0	10,897	371	8,671	1,855	0

(a) **What will be the FOUR entries in the general ledger?**

General ledger

Account name		Amount £	Debit	Credit
	▼			
	▼			
	▼			
	▼			

Drop-down list:

Bank
Cash
Cash purchases
Cash sales
Purchases ledger control
Rent received
Sales ledger control
Trade payables
Trade receivables
VAT

One of the bank receipts from trade receivables was from Finola Lynch for £1,266.

(b) **What will be the entry in the sales ledger?**

Sales ledger

Account name	Amount £	Debit	Credit
▼			

Drop-down list:

Bank
Finola Lynch
Gold
Purchases
Purchases ledger
Purchases ledger control
Sales
Sales ledger
Sales ledger control
Trade payables
Trade receivables

Task 5 (20 marks)

Gold maintains a petty cash-book as a book of prime entry and part of the double entry bookkeeping system. The imprest level of £130 is restored at the beginning of each month. This is a summary of petty cash transactions to be entered in the petty cash-book on 30 June.

Fuel purchased for delivery van – £42.00 including VAT

Desk lamp purchased – £18.30 (VAT not applicable)

(a) **Enter the above transactions into the partially completed petty cash-book below.**

(b) **Total the petty cash-book and show the balance carried down at 30 June.**

Petty cash-book

Date 20XX	Details	Amount £	Date 20XX	Details	Amount £	VAT £	Motor Expenses £	Office Expenses £
1 Jun	Balance b/f	51.58	19 Jun	Motor oil	26.40	4.40	22.00	
1 Jun	Cash from bank	78.42	30 Jun	▼				
			30 Jun	▼				
		_____	30 Jun	▼	_____	_____	_____	
	Total	130.00		Total				

Drop-down list:

Balance b/f
Balance c/d
Desk lamp
Motor expenses
Motor fuel
Office expenses
VAT

(c) **What will be the THREE accounts in the general ledger that will record the petty cash payments?**

General ledger accounts	
Desk lamp	☐
Motor expenses	☐
Motor fuel	☐
Motor oil	☐
Office expenses	☐
Petty cash-book	☐
Petty cash control	☐
VAT	☐

During July, two payments were made of £22.67 and £31.14. This is the debit side of the petty cash-book at the beginning of August.

(d) **Enter the balance brought down on 1 August.**

(e) **Enter the amount of cash that will be withdrawn from the bank to restore the imprest level.**

Petty cash-book – debit side

Date 20XX	Details	Amount £
1 Aug	Balance b/d	
1 Aug	Cash from bank	

These are the notes and coins that are now in the petty cash box.

Notes and coins
3 × £20 notes
13 × £5 notes
2 × £1 coins
1 × 50p coins
8 × 20p coins
9 × 10p coins

(f)   **What is the total amount of cash in the petty cash box?**

£ [   ]

(g)   **Does the amount of cash in the petty cash box reconcile with the petty cash-book?**

Yes	☐
No	☐

Task 6 (20 marks)

Below is a list of balances to be transferred to the trial balance.

Place the figures in the debit or credit column, as appropriate, and total each column.

Do not enter figures with decimal places in this task and do not enter a zero in the empty column.

Trial balance as at 30 June

Account name	Amount £	Debit £	Credit £
Administration expenses	2,054		
Capital	23,633		
Cash at bank	1,633		
Cash sales	10,742		
Commission received	725		
Fittings and equipment	32,955		
Heat and light	1,672		
Inventories	3,828		
Loan from investor	6,000		
Maintenance costs	1,818		
Purchases	199,789		
Purchases ledger control	76,427		
Purchases returns	6,825		
Sales	236,012		
Sales ledger control	89,216		
Travel costs	1,044		
VAT (owing from HM Revenue & Customs)	10,421		
Wages and salaries	15,934		
Totals			

Task 7 (15 marks)

Shown below is a statement of account received from Cooper and Crow, a credit supplier, and Cooper and Crow's account in Gold's purchases ledger.

Cooper and Crow
14 Winfield Road, Darton, DF15 8RL

STATEMENT OF ACCOUNT

To: Gold   30 June 20XX

Date 20XX	Invoice/credit note number	Details	Amount £
1 Apr	3106	Goods	1,221
5 Apr	132	Goods returned	200
12 Apr	3130	Goods	1,760
15 May	3144	Goods	1,002
1 Jun	3156	Goods	864

Cooper and Crow

Date 20XX	Details	Amount £	Date 20XX	Details	Amount £
5 Apr	Credit note 132	200	1 Apr	Invoice 3106	1,221
30 Apr	Balance c/d	3,701	10 Apr	Invoice 3121	920
			12 Apr	Invoice 3130	1,760
	Total	3,901		Total	3,901
31 May	Balance c/d	4,968	1 May	Balance b/d	3,701
			7 May	Invoice 3139	265
			15 May	Invoice 3144	1,002
	Total	4,968		Total	4,968
30 Jun	Balance c/d	6,282	1 Jun	Balance b/d	4,968
			1 Jun	Invoice 3156	864
			30 Jun	Invoice 3160	450
	Total	6,282		Total	6,282

(a) **Show which THREE transactions are missing from the statement of account by selecting the relevant invoice or credit note below.**

Transactions				
Invoice 3106	Invoice 3121	Invoice 3130	Invoice 3139	Invoice 3144
Invoice 3156	Invoice 3160	Credit note 132		

Gold must decide what payment to make to Cooper and Crow.

(b) **Calculate the payment options shown below.**

Payment options	£
If Gold pays all of the amounts shown on the statement of account from Cooper and Crow, what will be the amount paid?	
If Gold pays the amount shown as outstanding in the purchases ledger for April, what will be the amount paid?	
If Gold pays all of the amounts shown as outstanding in the purchases ledger, what will be the amount paid?	

On 12 July Gold ordered goods from Cooper and Crow who agreed a 10% trade discount and payment terms of 30 days net. The goods were delivered on 15 July and the invoice and goods received note are shown below.

Invoice

Cooper and Crow 14 Winfield Road, Darton, DF15 8RL VAT Registration No. 398 3877 00

To: Gold	Invoice No. 3172	15 June 20XX
		£
350 product code CC45 @ £0.60 each		210.00
VAT @ 20%		42.00
Total		252.00

Terms: Cash on delivery

Goods received note

Gold
Goods received note GRN442
15 July 20XX
Received from: Cooper and Crow
350 product code CC45 in good condition

(c) **Refer to the information above and the goods received note and identify any discrepancies on the invoice by matching the boxes in the left-hand column to the appropriate box right-hand column.**

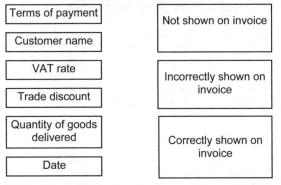

Terms of payment		Not shown on invoice
Customer name		
VAT rate		Incorrectly shown on invoice
Trade discount		
Quantity of goods delivered		Correctly shown on invoice
Date		

(d) **What should have been the correct amounts of the invoice?**

Net amount £	VAT amount £	Gross amount £

Task 8 (15 marks)

On 2 July Gold received a cheque from a credit customer Jet Ltd, together with the document shown below.

Jet Ltd
22 Ravenscourt Street
Darton, DF15 0MX

To: Gold   30 June 20XX

Cheque enclosed in payment of:

Invoice date 20XX	Invoice number	Invoice total £	Details of payment
13 June	3177	369	Paid in full
20 June	3201	421	Discount taken
23 June	3210	565	Paid in full
26 June	3225	86	Discount taken

(a)   What is the name of this document?

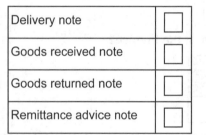

Delivery note	☐
Goods received note	☐
Goods returned note	☐
Remittance advice note	☐

Jet Ltd takes a 2% settlement discount if payment is received by Gold within 10 days of the date of invoice.

(b)   Show whether or not each invoice has been paid correctly.

Invoice date 20XX	Invoice number	Invoice total £	Details of payment	Paid correctly	NOT paid correctly
13 June	3177	369	Paid in full	☐	☐
20 June	3201	421	Discount taken	☐	☐
23 June	3210	565	Paid in full	☐	☐
26 June	3225	86	Discount taken	☐	☐

On 12 July Gold received the following purchase order from Jet Ltd, customer account code JET03. The goods were delivered the following day. The customer has been offered a 4% trade discount and a 2% settlement discount for payment within 10 days.

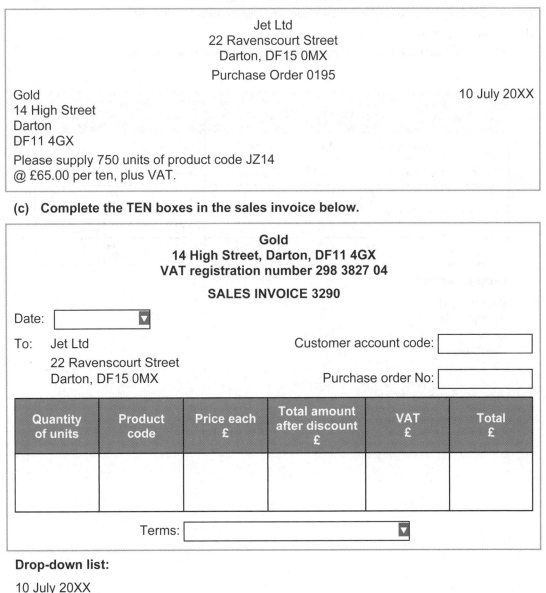

Jet Ltd
22 Ravenscourt Street
Darton, DF15 0MX

Purchase Order 0195

Gold   10 July 20XX
14 High Street
Darton
DF11 4GX

Please supply 750 units of product code JZ14
@ £65.00 per ten, plus VAT.

(c) Complete the TEN boxes in the sales invoice below.

Gold
14 High Street, Darton, DF11 4GX
VAT registration number 298 3827 04

SALES INVOICE 3290

Date: [▼]

To: Jet Ltd   Customer account code: [   ]
       22 Ravenscourt Street
       Darton, DF15 0MX   Purchase order No: [   ]

Quantity of units	Product code	Price each £	Total amount after discount £	VAT £	Total £

Terms: [▼]

Drop-down list:

10 July 20XX
11 July 20XX
12 July 20XX
13 July 20XX

Net monthly account
30 days net
2% settlement discount for payment within 10 days
4% trade discount

Task 9 (15 marks)

The following account is in the sales ledger at the close of day on 30 June.

(a) Insert the balance carried down together with date and details.

(b) Insert the totals.

(c) Insert the balance brought down together with date and details.

Helga plc

Date 20XX	Details	Amount £	Date 20XX	Details	Amount £
1 Jun	Balance b/f	4,073	4 Jun	Cheque	2,645
17 Jun	Invoice 1412	3,219	23 Jun	Credit note 301	828
	▼	_____		▼	_____
	Total	══════		Total	══════
	▼			▼	

Drop-down list:

Balance b/d
Balance c/d
Gold
Helga plc

(d) **Complete the statement of account to be sent to Helga plc by:**

- Entering the amount of the balance brought forward into the final column
- Writing the individual date and details below into the first column
- Entering the outstanding amount after every transaction into the final column

STATEMENT OF ACCOUNT

Gold
14 High Street, Darton, DF11 4GX.

To: Helga plc

Date: 30 June 20XX

Date and details	Transaction amount £	Outstanding amount £
01 June 20XX – Balance b/f		
	2,645	
	3,219	
	828	

Date and details:

| 17 June 20XX – Invoice 1412 | 04 June 20XX – Cheque | 23 June 20XX – Credit note 301 |

Task 10 (15 marks)

It is important to understand the accounting equation.

(a) **Insert the correct answer to each of the questions below.**

Questions	£
If assets total £89,475 and liabilities total £66,127 what is the amount of capital?	
If liabilities total £123,890 and capital is £55,670 what is the amount of assets?	
If capital is £101,466 and assets total £176,333 what is the amount of liabilities?	

(b) **Show whether the items below are assets or liabilities by linking each left-hand box to the appropriate right-hand box.**

Items	Assets/Liabilities
Loan from an investor	Assets
Inventories	
VAT owing to HM Revenue & Customs	Liabilities
Office furniture	

At the start of the day Gold's assets and liabilities included the following items.

Assets and liabilities	£
Trade receivables	47,607
Trade payables	32,419
Cash at bank	4,791

During the day Gold received £10,765 from trade receivables and made payments of £12,798 to trade payables.

(c) **Complete the table below to show the amount of assets and liabilities at the end of the day.**

Assets and liabilities	£
Trade receivables	
Trade payables	
Cash at bank	

Payments made and received can be classified as capital expenditure, revenue expenditure, capital income or revenue income.

(d) Complete the sentences below.

A receipt of £5,000 for a cash sale is classified as [▼]

A payment of £3,399 for new windows is classified as [▼]

A payment of £2,500 for insurance is classified as [▼]

A receipt of £450 for the rental of office space is classified as [▼]

A payment of £1,845 to redecorate the office is classified as [▼]

Drop-down list:

capital expenditure.
revenue expenditure.
capital income.
revenue income.

AAT AQ2013 SAMPLE ASSESSMENT 2 PROCESSING BOOKKEEPING TRANSACTIONS

ANSWERS

Task 1 (15 marks)

Sales day-book

Date 20XX	Details	Customer account code	Invoice number	Total £	VAT £	Net £	Product AP £	Product AZ £
30 Jun	JJ Firth ▼	FIR06	4789	522.24	87.04	435.2	256	179.20

Sales returns day-book

Date 20XX	Details	Customer account code	Invoice number	Total £	VAT £	Net £	Product AP £	Product AZ £
30 Jun	Cox plc ▼	COX11	983	691.2	115.2	576	576	

Task 2 (15 marks)

(a) **Purchases ledger**

Account name	Amount £	Debit	Credit
Green and Co ▼	918	✓	
Kitty Cain ▼	1,344	✓	

(b) **General ledger**

Account name	Amount £	Debit	Credit
Purchases ledger control ▼	2,262	✓	
Purchases returns ▼	1,885		✓
VAT ▼	377		✓

BPP
LEARNING MEDIA

Task 3 (20 marks)

(a) **Cash book – debit side**

Details	Discounts £	Cash £	Bank £	VAT £	Trade receivables £	Cash sales £
Balance b/f		220				
Bob Sykes ▼		462		77		385
Lynch Ltd ▼	116		1,988		1,988	
Tara plc ▼	85		1,219		1,219	
Total	201	682	3,207	77	3,207	385

(b) £ [193] 682 – 489 = 193

(c) £ [–846] 1,146 + 3,207 – 2,907 = –846

- -

Task 4 (15 marks)

(a) **General ledger**

Account name	Amount £	Debit	Credit
VAT ▼	371		✓
Sales ledger control ▼	8,671		✓
Cash sales ▼	1,855		✓
Bank ▼	10,897	✓	

(b) **Sales ledger**

Account name	Amount £	Debit	Credit
Finola Lynch ▼	1,266		✓

- -

232

Task 5 (20 marks)

(a) – (b)

Petty cash-book

Date 20XX	Details	Amount £	Date 20XX	Details		Amount £	VAT £	Motor Expenses £	Office Expenses £
1 Jun	Balance b/f	51.58	19 Jun	Motor oil		26.40	4.40	22.00	
1 Jun	Cash from bank	78.42	30 Jun	Motor fuel	▼	42.00	7.00	35.00	
			30 Jun	Desk lamp	▼	18.30			18.30
			30 Jun	Balance c/d	▼	43.30			
	Total	130.00		Total		130	11.40	57.00	18.30

(c)

General ledger accounts	
Desk lamp	☐
Motor expenses	☑
Motor fuel	☐
Motor oil	☐
Office expenses	☑
Petty cash-book	☐
Petty cash control	☐
VAT	☑

(d) – (e)

Petty cash-book – debit side

Date 20XX	Details	Amount £
1 Aug	Balance b/d	76.19
1 Aug	Cash from bank	53.81

Cash from bank = £22.67 + £31.14 = £53.81

£130 – £53.81 = £76.19.

(f) £ 130

(g)

Yes	✓
No	

Task 6 (20 marks)

Trial balance as at 30 June

Account name	Amount £	Debit £	Credit £
Administration expenses	2,054	2,054	
Capital	23,633		23,633
Cash at bank	1,633	1,633	
Cash sales	10,742		10,742
Commission received	725		725
Fittings and equipment	32,955	32,955	
Heat and light	1,672	1,672	
Inventories	3,828	3,828	
Loan from investor	6,000		6,000
Maintenance costs	1,818	1,818	
Purchases	199,789	199,789	
Purchases ledger control	76,427		76,427
Purchases returns	6,825		6,825
Sales	236,012		236,012
Sales ledger control	89,216	89,216	
Travel costs	1,044	1,044	
VAT (owing from HM Revenue & Customs)	10,421	10,421	
Wages and salaries	15,934	15,934	
Totals		360,364	360,364

Task 7 (15 marks)

(a)

Transactions				
Invoice 3106	(Invoice 3121)	Invoice 3130	(Invoice 3139)	Invoice 3144
Invoice 3156	(Invoice 3160)	Credit note 132		

(b)

Payment options	£
If Gold pays all of the amounts shown on the statement of account from Cooper and Crow, what will be the amount paid?	4,647
If Gold pays the amount shown as outstanding in the purchases ledger for April, what will be the amount paid?	3,701
If Gold pays all of the amounts shown as outstanding in the purchases ledger, what will be the amount paid?	6,282

(c)

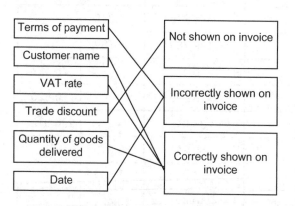

(d)

Net amount £	VAT amount £	Gross amount £
189	37.80	226.80

Task 8 (15 marks)

(a)

Delivery note	☐
Goods received note	☐
Goods returned note	☐
Remittance advice note	✓

(b)

Invoice date 20XX	Invoice number	Invoice total £	Details of payment	Paid correctly	NOT paid correctly
13 June	3177	369	Paid in full	✓	☐
20 June	3201	421	Discount taken	☐	✓
23 June	3210	565	Paid in full	☐	✓
26 June	3225	86	Discount taken	✓	☐

(c)

Gold
14 High Street, Darton, DF11 4GX
VAT registration number 298 3827 04

SALES INVOICE 3290

Date: 13 July 20XX ▼

To: Jet Ltd
22 Ravenscourt Street
Darton, DF15 0MX

Customer account code: JET03

Purchase order No: 0915

Quantity of units	Product code	Price each £	Total amount after discount £	VAT £	Total £
750	JZ14	6.50	4680.00	917.28	5597.28

Terms: 2% settlement discount for payment within 10 days ▼

Task 9 (15 marks)

(a) – (c)

Helga plc

Date 20XX	Details	Amount £	Date 20XX	Details	Amount £
1 Jun	Balance b/f	4,073	4 Jun	Cheque	2,645
17 Jun	Invoice 1412	3,219	23 Jun	Credit note 301	828
	▼	_____	30 Jun	Balance c/d ▼	3,819
	Total	7,292		Total	7,292
1 Jul	Balance b/d ▼	3,819		▼	

(d)

STATEMENT OF ACCOUNT

Gold
14 High Street, Darton, DF11 4GX.

To: Helga pic   Date: 30 June 20XX

Date and details	Transaction amount £	Outstanding amount £
01 June 20XX – Balance b/f		4,073
04 June 20XX – Cheque	2,645	1,428
17 June 20XX – Invoice 1412	3,219	4,647
23 June 20XX – Credit note 301	828	3,819

Task 10 (15 marks)

(a)

Questions	£
If assets total £89,475 and liabilities total £66,127, what is the amount of capital?	23,348 (89,475 – 66,127)
If liabilities total £123,890 and capital is £55,670, what is the amount of assets?	179,560 (123,890 + 55,670)
If capital is £101,466 and assets total £176,333, what is the amount of liabilities?	74,867 (176,355 – 101,466)

Asset – liability = capital

(b)

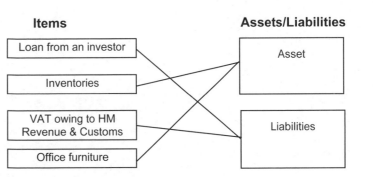

(c)

Assets and liabilities	£
Trade receivables	36,842
Trade payables	19,621
Cash at bank	2,758

(d)

A receipt of £5,000 for a cash sale is classified as | revenue income. ▼ |

A payment of £3,399 for new windows is classified as | capital expenditure. ▼ |

A payment of £2,500 for insurance is classified as | revenue expenditure. ▼ |

A receipt of £450 for the rental of office space is classified as | revenue income. ▼ |

A payment of £1,845 to redecorate the office is classified as | revenue expenditure. ▼ |

BPP PRACTICE ASSESSMENT 1
PROCESSING BOOKKEEPING
TRANSACTIONS

Time allowed: 2 hours

Processing Bookkeeping Transactions BPP practice assessment 1

Task 1

Purchases invoices have been checked and partially entered in the purchases day book, as shown below.

(a) **Complete the entries in the purchases day book by inserting the appropriate figures for each invoice.**

(b) **Total the last five columns of the purchases day book.**

Purchases day book

Date 20XX	Details	Invoice number	Total £	VAT £	Net £	Purchases £	Expenses £
30 Jun	Webble Ltd	76238		600		3,000	
30 Jun	Griddo plc	12522	288				240
30 Jun	Antic & Co	0938	816		680	680	
	Totals						

Trappic Ltd codes all purchase invoices with a supplier code AND a general ledger code. A selection of the codes used is given below.

Supplier	Supplier Code
Bridgend plc	BRI12
Distinct Ltd	DIS53
Finish Clear & Co	FIN09
Hepplewhite Clean Ltd	HEP76
Mirrors and Glass Ltd	MIR22
Item	**General Ledger Code**
Cleaning fluids	GL234
Mops and buckets	GL237
Brushes	GL240
Cloths	GL244
Protective clothing	GL248

This is an invoice received from a supplier.

Distinct Ltd	
89 Northcourt Road, Arbuckle AR5 3VB	
VAT Registration No. 837 4777 33	

Trappic Ltd
8 Highview Road
Arbuckle
AR7 4LX

22 July 20XX

10 mops with buckets @ £12.60 each	£126.00
VAT @ 20%	£ 25.20
Total	£151.20

(c) **Select which codes would be used to code this invoice.**

Supplier code	▼
General ledger code	▼

Picklist:

BRI12
DIS53
FIN09
HEP76
MIR22
GL234
GL237
GL240
GL244
GL248

(d) **Why is it necessary to use a supplier code?**

▼

Picklist:

To help trace relevant information quickly and easily
To help when ordering an item
To help find the total amount of purchases
To help when storing an item of inventory

Task 2

The following transactions all took place on 30 June and have been entered into the sales day book as shown below. No entries have yet been made into the ledger system.

Sales day book

Date 20XX	Details	Invoice number	Total £	VAT £	Net £
30 Jun	Trilby & Co	5264	3,936	656	3,280
30 Jun	R Strang Ltd	5265	1,776	296	1,480
30 Jun	Edwards plc	5266	12,528	2,088	10,440
30 Jun	Middleton Sumner Ltd	5267	7,152	1,192	5,960
	Totals		25,392	4,232	21,160

(a) **What will be the entries in the sales ledger?**

Sales ledger

Account name	Amount £	Debit ✓	Credit ✓
▼			
▼			
▼			
▼			

Picklist:

Edwards plc
Middleton Sumner Ltd
Purchases
Purchases ledger control
Purchases returns
R Strang Ltd
Sales
Sales ledger control
Sales returns
Trilby & Co
VAT

(b) **What will be the entries in the general ledger?**

General ledger

Account name	Amount £	Debit ✓	Credit ✓
▼			
▼			
▼			

Picklist:

Edwards plc
Middleton Sumner Ltd
Purchases
Purchases ledger control
Purchases returns
R Strang Ltd
Sales
Sales ledger control
Sales returns
Trilby & Co
VAT

The following credit transactions all took place on 30 June and have been entered into the purchases returns day book as shown below. No entries have yet been made in the ledgers.

Purchases returns day book

Date 20XX	Details	Credit note number	Total £	VAT @ 20% £	Net £
30 June	Bingley & Co	09374	672	112	560
30 June	Arkwright Ltd	CN5426	2,208	368	1,840
	Totals		2,880	480	2,400

(c) **What will be the entries in the purchases ledger?**

Purchases ledger

Account name	Amount £	Debit ✓	Credit ✓
▼			
▼			

Picklist:

Arkwright Ltd
Bingley & Co
Purchases
Purchases ledger control
Purchases returns
Sales
Sales ledger control
Sales returns
VAT

(d) **What will be the entries in the general ledger?**

General ledger

Account name	Amount £	Debit ✓	Credit ✓
▼			
▼			
▼			

Picklist:

Arkwright Ltd
Bingley & Co
Purchases
Purchases ledger control
Purchases returns
Sales
Sales ledger control
Sales returns
VAT

Task 3

Russell Hardware has made five payments which are to be entered in its cash book.

Receipts for payments

Received cash with thanks for goods bought. From Russell Hardware, a customer without a credit account. Net £40 VAT £8 Total £48 *Cranula Ltd*	Received cash with thanks for goods bought. From Russell Hardware, a customer without a credit account. Net £240 VAT £48 Total £288 *Gesteor & Co*	Received cash with thanks for goods bought. From Russell Hardware, a customer without a credit account. Net £167 (No VAT) *S Ransome*

Cheque book counterfoils

Weston Ltd (Purchase ledger account WES001) £1,452 (Note: Have taken £30 settlement discount) 109923	Stationery Shop Ltd (We have no credit account with this supplier) £240 including VAT 109924

(a) **Enter the details from the three receipts and two cheque book stubs into the credit side of the cash book shown below and total each column.**

Cash book – credit side

Details	Discount £	Cash £	Bank £	VAT £	Trade payables £	Cash purchases £	Stationery £
Balance b/f			135				
Cranula Ltd							
Gesteor & Co							
S Ransome							
Weston Ltd							
Stationery Shop Ltd							
Total							

There are also two cheques from credit customers to be entered in Russell Hardware's cash book:

Middle Firth Ltd   £673
High Tops plc   £1,092 (this customer has taken a £50 discount)

(b) **Enter the above details into the debit side of the cash book and total each column.**

Cash book – debit side

Details	Discount £	Cash £	Bank £	Trade receivables £
Balance b/f		629		
Middle Firth Ltd				
High Tops plc				
Total				

(c) **Using your answers to (a) and (b), above calculate the cash balance.**

£ [   ]

(d) **Using your answers to (a) and (b), above calculate the bank balance.**

£ [   ]

(e) **Will the bank balance calculated in (d) above be a debit or credit balance?**

	✓
Debit	
Credit	

Task 4

A business's cash book is both a book of prime entry and part of the double entry system. The following transactions all took place on 30 June and have been entered in the debit side of the cash book as shown below. No entries have yet been made in the ledgers.

Cash book – debit side

Date 20XX	Details	Cash £	Bank £	VAT £	Cash sales £	Trade receivables £
30 Jun	Henderson & Co		7,349			7,349
30 Jun	Cash sale	426		71	355	

(a) **What will be the entry in the sales ledger?**

Sales ledger

Account name	Amount £	Debit ✓	Credit ✓
▼			

Picklist:

Cash
Bank
Henderson & Co
Purchases ledger control
Sales
Sales ledger control
VAT

(b) **What will be the THREE entries in the general ledger?**

General ledger

Account name	Amount £	Debit ✓	Credit ✓
▼			
▼			
▼			

Picklist:

Cash
Bank
Henderson & Co
Purchases ledger control
Sales
Sales ledger control
VAT

The following transactions all took place on 30 June and have been entered in the credit side of the cash book as shown below. No entries have yet been made in the ledgers.

Cash book – credit side

Date 20XX	Details	Discounts £	Bank £
30 Jun	Balance b/d		575
30 Jun	Resto plc	10	282

(c) **What will be the THREE entries in the general ledger?**

General ledger

Account name	Amount £	Debit ✓	Credit ✓
▼			
▼			
▼			

Picklist:

Balance b/d
Balance c/d
Bank
Discounts allowed
Discounts received
Purchases ledger control
Resto plc
Sales ledger control
VAT

Trappic Ltd maintains a petty cash book as both a book of prime entry and part of the double entry bookkeeping system. The following transactions all took place on 30 June and have been entered in the petty cash book as shown below. No entries have yet been made in the general ledger.

Petty cash book

Date 20XX	Details	Total £	Date 20XX	Details	Total £	VAT £	Motor expenses £	Travel £	Office expenses £
30 Jun	Balance b/d	75.00	30 Jun	Tea/biscuits	7.89				7.89
			30 Jun	Train fare	23.40			23.40	
			30 Jun	Paper	48.00	8.00			40.00
30 Jun	Bank	225.00	30 Jun	Oil for car	21.60	3.60	18.00		
			30 Jun	Balance c/d	199.11				
		300.00			300.00	11.60	18.00	23.40	47.89

(d) **What will be the FIVE entries in the general ledger?**

General ledger

Account name	Amount £	Debit ✓	Credit ✓
▼			
▼			
▼			
▼			
▼			

Picklist:

Balance b/d
Balance c/d
Bank
Motor expenses
Office expenses
Oil for car
Paper
Tea/biscuits
Train fare
Travel
Petty cash book
VAT

Task 5

This is a summary of petty cash payments made by Russell Hardware.

Office Supplies Ltd paid	£26.00 (plus VAT)
Post Office paid	£12.00 (no VAT)
RN Travel paid	£33.00 (no VAT)

(a) **Enter the above transactions, in the order in which they are shown, in the petty cash book.**

(b) **Total the petty cash book and show the balance carried down.**

Petty cash book

Debit side		Credit side					
Details	Amount £	Details	Amount £	VAT £	Postage £	Travel £	Office expenses £
Balance b/f	250.00	▼					
		▼					
		▼					
		▼					
Total		Total					

Picklist:

Amount
Balance b/d
Balance c/d
Details
Postage
Post Office
Office expenses
Office Supplies Ltd
RN Travel
Travel
VAT

Part way through the month the petty cash account had a balance of £98.40. The cash in the petty cash box was checked and the following notes and coins were there.

Notes and coins	£
3 × £20 notes	60.00
1 × £10 note	10.00
1 × £5 note	5.00
13 × £1 coins	13.00
5 × 50p coins	2.50
21 × 10p coins	2.10
12 × 5p coins	0.60

(c) **Reconcile the cash amount in the petty cash box with the balance on the petty cash account.**

Amount in petty cash box	£	
Balance on petty cash account	£	
Difference	£	

At the end of the month the cash in the petty cash box was £11.95.

(d) **Complete the petty cash reimbursement document below to restore the imprest amount of £250.**

Petty cash reimbursement		
Date: 31.07.20XX		
Amount required to restore the cash in the petty cash box	£	

Task 6

Below is a list of balances to be transferred to the trial balance as at 30 June.

Place the figures in the debit or credit column, as appropriate, and total each column. Do not enter figures with decimal places in this task and do not enter a zero in the empty column.

Account name	Amount £	Debit £	Credit £
Machinery	15,000		
Inventory	3,907		
Cash at bank	1,342		
Petty cash	150		
Sales ledger control	9,486		
Purchases ledger control	4,003		
VAT (owing to HM Revenue & Customs)	1,880		
Capital	10,000		
Loan from bank	2,500		
Sales	86,262		
Sales returns	1,256		
Purchases	43,278		
Purchases returns	295		
Discounts received	987		
Discounts allowed	628		
Salaries	21,965		
Motor expenses	1,025		
Office expenses	1,234		
Premises costs	2,833		
Marketing expenses	765		
Travel	911		
Telephone	1,260		
Heat and light	1,387		
Rental income	500		
Totals			

Task 7

A supply of cleaning fluid has been delivered to Trappic Ltd by OMKG Chemicals. The purchase order sent from Trappic Ltd, and the invoice from OMKG Chemicals, are shown below.

**Trappic Ltd
8 Highview Road
Arbuckle
AR7 4LX**

Purchase Order No. 637821

To: OMKG Chemicals

Date: 15 July 20XX

Please supply 1000 litres cleaning fluid product code 7638XX
Purchase price: £8.00 per 10 litres, plus VAT
Discount: less 15% trade discount, as agreed

**OMKG Chemicals
76 Grange Road, Arbuckle AR1 0HJ
VAT Registration No. 653 9922 33**

Invoice No. 76383

Trappic Ltd
8 Highview Road
Arbuckle
AR7 4LX

22 July 20XX

1,000 litres cleaning fluid product code 7638XX @ £0.80 per litre	£800.00
Less trade discount at 12.5%	£100.00
	£700.00
VAT @ 20%	£140.00
Total	£840.00

Terms: 30 days net

(a) **Check the invoice against the purchase order and answer the following questions.**

	Yes ✓	No ✓
Has the correct purchase price of the cleaning fluid been charged?		
Has the correct discount been applied?		
What would be the VAT amount charged if the invoice was correct?	£	
What would be the total amount charged if the invoice was correct?	£	

Shown below is a statement of account received from a credit supplier, and the supplier's account as shown in the purchases ledger of Trappic Ltd.

Lemonfresh Ltd
90 West Street
Arbuckle
AR4 8AM

To: Trappic Ltd
8 Highview Road
Arbuckle
AR7 4LX

STATEMENT OF ACCOUNT

Date 20XX	Invoice Number	Details	Invoice amount £	Cheque amount £	Balance £
1 May	1267	Goods	180		180
3 June	1387	Goods	230		410
7 June	1422	Goods	290		700
10 June	1498	Goods	800		1,500
16 June		Cheque		510	990

Lemonfresh Ltd

Date 20XX	Details	Amount £	Date 20XX	Details	Amount £
16 June	Bank	510	1 May	Purchases	180
16 June	Discount	10	3 June	Purchases	230
			7 June	Purchases	290

(b) **Which item is missing from the statement of account from Lemonfresh Ltd?**

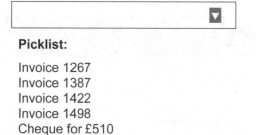

Picklist:

Invoice 1267
Invoice 1387
Invoice 1422
Invoice 1498
Cheque for £510
Discount for £10

(c) **Which item is missing from the supplier account in Trappic Ltd's purchases ledger?**

Picklist:

Invoice 1267
Invoice 1387
Invoice 1422
Invoice 1498
Cheque for £510
Discount for £10

(d) **Assuming any differences between the statement of account from Lemonfresh Ltd and the supplier account in Trappic Ltd's purchases ledger are simply due to omission errors, what is the amount owing to Lemonfresh Ltd?**

£

(e) Trappic Ltd prepares a remittance advice note in respect of Lemonfresh Ltd.

Which of the following statements is true?

	✓
The remittance advice note will be sent to the customer to advise them of the amount being paid	
The remittance advice note will be sent to the supplier's bank to advise them of the amount being paid	
The remittance advice note will be sent to the supplier to advise them of the amount being paid	
The remittance advice note will be sent to the accounts department at Lemonfresh Ltd to request that a cheque is raised	

Task 8

On 5 July Trappic Ltd delivered the following goods to a credit customer, Nemesis Ltd.

Trappic Ltd

8 Highview Road
Arbuckle
AR7 4LX

Delivery note No. 8793
05 July 20XX

Nemesis Ltd   Customer account code: NEM893
36 Ventnor Road
Arbuckle
AR7 9LC

200 polishing cloths, product code C420.

The list price of the goods was £0.50 per cloth plus VAT. Nemesis Ltd is to be given a 10% trade discount and a 4% early settlement discount.

(a) **Complete the invoice below.**

Trappic Ltd
8 Highview Road
Arbuckle
AR7 4LX

VAT Registration No. 782 8723 23

Nemesis Ltd   Customer account code: NEM893

36 Ventnor Road
Arbuckle
AR7 9LC
Date: 6 July 20XX

Invoice No: 67282
Delivery note number: 8793

Quantity of goods	Product code	Total list price £	Net amount after trade discount £	VAT £	Gross £

Trappic Ltd offers each customer a discount of 5% if any order amounts to £1,000 or over.

(b) **What is the name of this type of discount?**

▼

Picklist:

Bulk discount
Settlement discount
Trade discount

The account shown below is in the sales ledger of Trappic Ltd. A cheque for £2,311 has now been received from this customer.

Sibley & Co

Date 20XX	Details	Amount £	Date 20XX	Details	Amount £
1 May	Balance b/d	2,897	2 June	Sales returns credit note 5530	173
3 June	Sales invoice 66100	2,556	25 June	Bank	2,724
28 June	Sales Invoice 66800	2,453	26 June	Sales returns credit note 5570	245

(c) **Which outstanding item has not been included in the payment of £2,311?**

▼

Picklist:

Balance b/d
Sales invoice 66100
Sales invoice 66800
Bank
Sales returns credit note 5530
Sales returns credit note 5570

An invoice is being prepared to be sent to Sibley & Co for £760.00 plus VAT of £144.40. A settlement discount of 5% will be offered for payment within 10 days.

(d) **What is the amount Trappic Ltd should receive if payment is made within 10 days?**

£	

(e) **What is the amount Trappic Ltd should receive if payment is NOT made within 10 days?**

£	

Task 9

The following two accounts are in the general ledger at the close of day on 30 June.

For each account:

(a) **Insert the balance carried down together with date and details.**
(b) **Insert the totals.**
(c) **Insert the balance brought down together with date and details.**

Heat and light

Date 20XX	Details	Amount £	Date 20XX	Details	Amount £
01 Jun	Balance b/d	2,039		▼	
26 Jun	Purchases ledger control	348		▼	
	▼			▼	
	Total			Total	
	▼			▼	

Picklist:

Balance b/d
Balance c/d
Bank
Purchases ledger control

Sales

Date 20XX	Details	Amount £	Date 20XX	Details	Amount £
	▼		01 Jun	Balance b/d	32,986
	▼		22 Jun	Bank	750
	▼			▼	
	Total			Total	
	▼			▼	

Picklist:

Balance b/d
Balance c/d
Bank
Sales ledger control

The following is a summary of Trappic Ltd's transactions with Quemix Ltd, a new credit customer.

£1,020 re invoice 67300 of 11 July
£987 re invoice 67400 of 19 July
£48 re credit note 5640 of 24 July
£2,967 re invoice 67500 of 28 July
Cheque for £1,020 received 31 July

(d) **Complete the statement of account below.**

Trappic Ltd
8 Highview Road
Arbuckle
AR7 4LX

To: Quemix Ltd　　　　　　　　　　　　　　　　　　　Date: 31 July 20XX

Date 20XX	Details	Transaction amount £	Outstanding amount £
11 July			
19 July			
24 July			
28 July			
31 July			

Task 10

It is important to understand the difference between capital expenditure, revenue expenditure, capital income and revenue income.

(a) **Select one option in each instance below to show whether, in relation to Trappic Ltd, the item will be capital expenditure, revenue expenditure, capital income or revenue income.**

Item	Capital expenditure ✓	Revenue expenditure ✓	Capital income ✓	Revenue income ✓
Purchase of mops and buckets for resale				
Receipt from sale of an item of Trappic Ltd's machinery				
Purchase of delivery vehicle				
Cash purchases				
Payments to credit suppliers				
Sale of goods for cash				

Financial accounting is based upon the accounting equation.

(b) **Show whether the following statements are True or False.**

	True ✓	False ✓
Income less expenditure is equal to assets		
Capital plus liabilities are equal to assets		
Liabilities equal assets plus capital		

(c) **Classify each of the following items as an asset, a liability or capital.**

Item	Asset, liability or capital?
Money contributed by the owners	▼
Bank overdraft	▼
Petty cash	▼

Picklist:

Asset
Liability
Capital

BPP PRACTICE ASSESSMENT 1
PROCESSING BOOKKEEPING
TRANSACTIONS

ANSWERS

Processing Bookkeeping Transactions BPP practice assessment 1

Task 1

(a) – (b)

Purchases day book

Date 20XX	Details	Invoice number	Total £	VAT £	Net £	Purchases £	Expenses £
30 Jun	Webble Ltd	76238	3,600	600	3,000	3,000	
30 Jun	Griddo plc	I2522	288	48	240		240
30 Jun	Antic & Co	0938	816	136	680	680	
	Totals		4,704	784	3,920	3,680	240

(c)

Supplier code	DIS53
General ledger code	GL237

(d) The correct answer is: to help trace relevant information quickly and easily

....

Task 2

(a)

Sales ledger

Account name	Amount £	Debit ✓	Credit ✓
Edwards plc	12,528	✓	
Middleton Sumner Ltd	7,152	✓	
R Strang Ltd	1,776	✓	
Trilby & Co	3,936	✓	

(b)

General ledger

Account name	Amount £	Debit ✓	Credit ✓
Sales	21,160		✓
Sales ledger control	25,392	✓	
VAT	4,232		✓

(c)

Purchases ledger

Account name	Amount £	Debit ✓	Credit ✓
Arkwright Ltd	2,208	✓	
Bingley & Co	672	✓	

(d)

General ledger

Account name	Amount £	Debit ✓	Credit ✓
Purchases ledger control	2,880	✓	
Purchases returns	2,400		✓
VAT	480		✓

Task 3

(a)

Cash book – credit side

Details	Discount £	Cash £	Bank £	VAT £	Trade payables £	Cash purchases £	Stationery £
Balance b/f			135				
Cranula Ltd		48		8		40	
Gesteor & Co		288		48		240	
S Ransome		167				167	
Weston Ltd	30		1,452		1,452		
Stationery Shop Ltd		.	240	40			200
Total	30	503	1,827	96	1,452	447	200

(b)

Cash book – debit side

Details	Discount £	Cash £	Bank £	Trade receivables £
Balance b/f		629		
Middle Firth Ltd			673	673
High Tops plc	50		1,092	1,092
Total	50	629	1,765	1,765

(c) The correct answer is: £126 (629 – 503 = 126)

(d) The correct answer is: £62 (1,765 – 1,827)

(e) The correct answer is: Credit

269

Task 4

(a)

Sales ledger

Account name	Amount £	Debit ✓	Credit ✓
Henderson & Co	7,349		✓

(b)

General ledger

Account name	Amount £	Debit ✓	Credit ✓
Sales ledger control	7,349		✓
Sales	355		✓
VAT	71		✓

(c)

General ledger

Account name	Amount £	Debit ✓	Credit ✓
Purchases ledger control	282	✓	
Purchases ledger control	10	✓	
Discounts received	10		✓

(d)

General ledger

Account name	Amount £	Debit ✓	Credit ✓
Bank	225.00		✓
Motor expenses	18.00	✓	
Office expenses	47.89	✓	
Travel	23.40	✓	
VAT	11.60	✓	

Task 5

(a) – (b)

Petty cash book

Debit side		Credit side					
Details	Amount £	Details	Amount £	VAT £	Postage £	Travel £	Office expenses £
Balance b/f	250.00	Office Supplies Ltd	31.20	5.20			26.00
		Post Office	12.00		12.00		
		RN Travel	33.00			33.00	
		Balance c/d	173.80				
	250.00		250.00	5.20	12.00	33.00	26.00

(c)

Amount in petty cash box	£	93.20
Balance on petty cash account	£	98.40
Difference	£	5.20

(d)

Petty cash reimbursement		
Date: 31.07.20XX		
Amount required to restore the cash in the petty cash box	£	238.05

Task 6

Account name	Amount £	Debit £	Credit £
Machinery	15,000	15,000	
Inventory	3,907	3,907	
Cash at bank	1,342	1,342	
Petty cash	150	150	
Sales ledger control	9,486	9,486	
Purchases ledger control	4,003		4,003
VAT (owing to HM Revenue & Customs)	1,880		1,880
Capital	10,000		10,000
Loan from bank	2,500		2,500
Sales	86,262		86,262
Sales returns	1,256	1,256	
Purchases	43,278	43,278	
Purchases returns	295		295
Discounts received	987		987
Discounts allowed	628	628	
Salaries	21,965	21,965	
Motor expenses	1,025	1,025	
Office expenses	1,234	1,234	
Premises costs	2,833	2,833	
Marketing expenses	765	765	
Travel	911	911	
Telephone	1,260	1,260	
Heat and light	1,387	1,387	
Rental income	500		500
Totals		106,427	106,427

Task 7

(a) VAT: (800 – (800 × 15/100)) × 20/100 = 136

Total: (800 – (800 × 15/100)) + 136 = 816

	Yes ✓	No ✓
Has the correct purchase price of the cleaning fluid been charged?	✓	
Has the correct discount been applied?		✓
What would be the VAT amount charged if the invoice was correct?	£	136
What would be the total amount charged if the invoice was correct?	£	816

(b) The correct answer is: discount for £10

(c) The correct answer is: invoice 1498

(d) The correct answer is: £980

£990 – £10 = £980

(e) The correct answer is: the remittance advice note will be sent to the supplier to advise them of the amount being paid

Task 8

(a) VAT: (90 – (90 × 4/100)) × 20/100 = £17.28

<table>
<tr><td colspan="6">Trappic Ltd
8 Highview Road
Arbuckle
AR7 4LX</td></tr>
<tr><td colspan="6" style="text-align:center">VAT Registration No. 782 8723 23</td></tr>
<tr><td colspan="3">Nemesis Ltd
36 Ventnor Road
Arbuckle
AR7 9LC

Invoice No: 67282
Delivery note number: 8793</td><td colspan="3">Customer account code: NEM893

Date: 6 July 20XX</td></tr>
<tr><th>Quantity of goods</th><th>Product code</th><th>Total list price £</th><th>Net amount after trade discount £</th><th>VAT £</th><th>Gross £</th></tr>
<tr><td>200</td><td>C420</td><td>100.00</td><td>90.00</td><td>17.28</td><td>107.28</td></tr>
</table>

(b) The correct answer is: bulk discount

(c) The correct answer is: sales invoice 66800

(d) The correct answer is: £866.40

Working

(£760.00 × 95%) + £144.40 = £866.40

(e) The correct answer is: £904.40

Working

(£760.00 + £144.40 = £904.40)

Task 9

(a) – (c)

Heat and light

Date 20XX	Details	Amount £	Date 20XX	Details	Amount £
01 Jun	Balance b/d	2,039			
26 Jun	Purchases ledger control	348			
			30 Jun	Balance c/d	2,387
	Total	2,387		Total	2,387
1 Jul	Balance b/d	2,387			

Sales

Date 20XX	Details	Amount £	Date 20XX	Details	Amount £
			01 Jun	Balance b/d	32,986
			22 Jun	Bank	750
30 Jun	Balance c/d	33,736			
	Total	33,736		Total	33,736
			1 Jul	Balance b/d	33,736

(d)

Trappic Ltd
8 Highview Road
Arbuckle
AR7 4LX

To: Quemix Ltd   Date: 31 July 20XX

Date 20XX	Details	Transaction amount £	Outstanding amount £
11 July	Invoice 67300	1,020	1,020
19 July	Invoice 67400	987	2,007
24 July	Credit note 5640	48	1,959
28 July	Invoice 67500	2,967	4,926
31 July	Cheque	1,020	3,906

Task 10

(a)

Item	Capital expenditure ✓	Revenue expenditure ✓	Capital income ✓	Revenue income ✓
Purchase of mops and buckets for resale		✓		
Receipt from sale of an item of Trappic Ltd's machinery			✓	
Purchase of delivery vehicle	✓			
Cash purchases		✓		
Payments to credit suppliers		✓		
Sale of goods for cash				✓

(b)

	True ✓	False ✓
Income less expenditure is equal to assets		✓
Capital plus liabilities are equal to assets	✓	
Liabilities equal assets plus capital		✓

(c)

Item	Asset, liability or capital?
Money contributed by the owners	Capital
Bank overdraft	Liability
Petty cash	Asset

BPP PRACTICE ASSESSMENT 2
PROCESSING BOOKKEEPING
TRANSACTIONS

Time allowed: 2 hours

Processing Bookkeeping Transactions BPP practice assessment 2

All answers should be rounded to the nearest penny unless otherwise instructed.

Task 1

Credit notes from suppliers have been checked and partially entered in the purchases returns day book, as shown below.

(a) **Complete the entries in the purchases returns day book by inserting the appropriate figures for each credit note.**

(b) **Total the last four columns of the purchases returns day book.**

Purchases returns day book

Date 20XX	Details	Credit note number	Total £	VAT £	Net £	Purchases returns £
30 Jun	Sindar Ltd	CN873		352		1,760
30 Jun	Premier Inc	02936	2,496			2,080
30 Jun	Bargain Parts plc	1092/22	144		120	
	Totals					

Hazelcombe & Co codes all purchase invoices with a supplier code AND a general ledger code. A selection of the codes used is given below.

Supplier	Supplier Code
Curran Mews Ltd	C783
Findlay & Co	F920
Gosling Ltd	G224
Meston plc	M029
Postlethwaite Brothers	P673

Item	General Ledger Code
Facings	GL956
Fixings	GL962
Leads	GL967
Lights	GL971
Pumps	GL975

This is an invoice received from a supplier.

Findlay & Co
98 Green Road, Luscombe LU9 0CV
VAT Registration No. 987 3666 237

Hazelcombe & Co
42 Turnstile Trading Estate
Luscombe
LU9 0FG

17 July 20XX

20 lights (product code 72836) @ £6.80 each	£136.00
VAT @ 20%	£27.20
Total	£163.20

(c) **Select which codes would be used to code this invoice.**

Supplier code	▼
General ledger code	▼

Picklist:

C783
F920
G224
GL956
GL962
GL967
GL971
GL975
M029
P673

(d) **Why is it necessary to use a general ledger code for different types of purchases?**

▼

Picklist:

To help identify the amount spent on a particular category of inventory
To help identify how much is owed to a supplier
To help identify when to re-order an item of inventory
To help find the total amount of purchases

Task 2

The following transactions all took place on 30 June and have been entered into the purchases day book as shown below. No entries have yet been made into the ledger system.

Purchases day book

Date 20XX	Details	Invoice number	Total £	VAT £	Net £
30 Jun	Osman Ltd	2764	2,688	448	2,240
30 Jun	Foster Brothers	I546/20	1,536	256	1,280
30 Jun	Lindemann plc	67383	5,328	888	4,440
30 Jun	Stoke Rows Ltd	412	3,840	640	3,200
	Totals		13,392	2,232	11,160

(a) **What will be the entries in the purchases ledger?**

Purchases ledger

Account name	Amount £	Debit ✓	Credit ✓
▼			
▼			
▼			
▼			

Picklist:

Foster Brothers
Lindemann plc
Purchases
Purchases ledger control
Purchases returns

Osman Ltd
Sales
Sales ledger control
Sales returns
Stoke Rows Ltd
VAT

(b) **What will be the entries in the general ledger?**

General ledger

Account name	Amount £	Debit ✓	Credit ✓
▼			
▼			
▼			

Picklist:

Foster Brothers
Lindemann plc
Purchases
Purchases ledger control
Purchases returns
Osman Ltd
Sales
Sales ledger control
Sales returns
Stoke Rows Ltd
VAT

The following credit transactions all took place on 30 June and have been entered into the sales returns day book as shown below. No entries have yet been made in the ledgers.

Sales returns day book

Date 20XX	Details	Credit note number	Total £	VAT £	Net £
30 June	Austen Knight plc	CN876	144	24	120
30 June	Tristram Steers & Co	CN877	2,832	472	2,360
	Totals		2,976	496	2,480

(c) **What will be the entries in the sales ledger?**

Sales ledger

Account name	Amount £	Debit ✓	Credit ✓
▼			
▼			

Picklist:

Austen Knight plc
Purchases
Purchases ledger control
Purchases returns
Sales
Sales ledger control
Sales returns
Tristram Steers & Co
VAT

(d) **What will be the entries in the general ledger?**

General ledger

Account name	Amount £	Debit ✓	Credit ✓
▼			
▼			
▼			

Picklist:

Austen Knight plc
Purchases
Purchases ledger control
Purchases returns
Sales
Sales ledger control
Sales returns
Tristram Steers & Co
VAT

Task 3

Finn Clothing has made five payments which are to be entered in its cash book.

Receipts for payments

Received cash with thanks for goods bought.	Received cash with thanks for goods bought.	Received cash with thanks for goods bought.
From Finn Clothing, a customer without a credit account.	From Finn Clothing, a customer without a credit account.	From Finn Clothing, a customer without a credit account.
Net £920 VAT £184 Total £1,104	Net £160 VAT £32 Total £192	Net £193 (No VAT)
Wisper & Co	*Forback Ltd*	*Cresswell plc*

Cheque book counterfoils

Lampetus Ltd (Purchases ledger account LAM001) £2,135 (Note: Have taken £25 settlement discount) 003456	GMG Maintenance Services (We have no credit account with this supplier) £426 including VAT 003457

(a) **Enter the details from the three receipts and two cheque book stubs into the credit side of the cash book shown below and total each column.**

Cash book – credit side

Details	Discount £	Cash £	Bank £	VAT £	Trade payables £	Cash purchases £	Maintenance £
Balance b/f			1,902				
Wisper & Co							
Forback Ltd							
Cresswell plc							
Lampetus Ltd							
GMG Maintenance Services							
Total							

There are also two cheques from credit customers to be entered in Finn Clothing's cash book:

Prickles & Co   £2,837
Dreston Proops   £3,299 (this customer has taken a £75 discount)

(b) **Enter the above details into the debit side of the cash book and total each column.**

Cash book – debit side

Details	Discount £	Cash £	Bank £	Trade receivables £
Balance b/f		1,593		
Prickles & Co				
Dreston Proops				
Total				

(c) **Using your answers to (a) and (b) above, calculate the cash balance.**

£ | |

(d) **Using your answers to (a) and (b) above, calculate the bank balance.**

£ | |

(e) **Will the bank balance calculated in (d) above be a debit or credit balance?**

	✓
Debit	
Credit	

Task 4

The cash book is part of the double entry system as well as a book of prime entry.

The following transactions in respect of trade receivables all took place on 30 June and have been entered in the debit side of the cash book as shown below. No entries have yet been made in the ledgers.

Cash book – debit side

Date 20XX	Details	Discounts £	Bank £
30 Jun	Gwendolin Ltd	15	643
30 Jun	Marcham & Co		2,309
	Total	15	2,952

(a) **What will be the THREE entries in the sales ledger?**

Sales ledger

Account name	Amount £	Debit ✓	Credit ✓
▼			
▼			
▼			

Picklist:

Bank
Discounts allowed
Discounts received
Gwendolin Ltd
Marcham & Co
Purchases
Purchases ledger control
Sales
Sales ledger control
VAT

(b) **What will be the THREE entries in the general ledger?**

General ledger

Account name	Amount £	Debit ✓	Credit ✓
▼			
▼			
▼			

Picklist:

Bank
Discounts allowed
Discounts received
Gwendolin Ltd
Marcham & Co
Purchases
Purchases ledger control
Sales
Sales ledger control
VAT

The following transactions took place on 30 June and has been entered in the credit side of the cash book as shown below. No entries have yet been made in the ledgers.

Cash book – credit side

Date 20XX	Details	Cash £	Bank £	VAT £	Cash purchases £	Trade payables £
30 Jun	Bradfield & Co		2,385			2,385
30 Jun	Cash purchase	240		40	200	

(c) **What will be the entry in the purchases ledger?**

Purchases ledger

Account name	Amount £	Debit ✓	Credit ✓
▼			

Picklist:

Bank
Bradfield & Co
Cash
Cash purchases
Discounts allowed
Discounts received
Purchases
Purchases ledger control
Sales
Sales ledger control
VAT

(d) **What will be the THREE entries in the general ledger?**

General ledger

Account name	Amount £	Debit ✓	Credit ✓
▼			
▼			
▼			

Picklist:

Bank
Bradfield & Co
Cash
Cash purchases
Discounts allowed
Discounts received
Purchases
Purchases ledger control
Sales
Sales ledger control
VAT

Task 5

This is a summary of petty cash payments made by Finn Clothing.

Quick Bus Company paid	£12.50 (no VAT)
Star's Stationery paid	£18.00 (plus VAT)
Post Office paid	£8.00 (no VAT)

(a) **Enter the above transactions, in the order in which they are shown, in the petty cash book below.**

(b) **Total the petty cash book and show the balance carried down.**

Petty cash book

Debit side		Credit side					
Details	Amount £	Details	Amount £	VAT £	Stationery £	Travel £	Postage £
Balance b/f	120.00	▼					
▼		▼					
▼		▼					
▼		▼					
▼		▼					

Picklist for line items:

Amount
Balance b/d
Balance c/d
Details
Postage
Post Office
Stationery
Star's Stationery
Quick Bus Company
Travel
VAT

Part way through the month the petty cash account had a balance of £81.26. The cash in the petty cash box was checked and the following notes and coins were there.

Notes and coins	£
2 × £20 notes	40.00
2 × £10 notes	20.00
2 × £5 notes	10.00
2 × £2 coins	4.00
3 × £1 coins	3.00
1 × 50p coins	0.50
4 × 10p coins	0.40
5 × 5p coins	0.25
19 × 1p coins	0.19

(c) **Reconcile the cash amount in the petty cash box with the balance on the petty cash account.**

Amount in petty cash box	£	
Balance on petty cash account	£	
Difference	£	

At the end of the month the cash in the petty cash box was £7.77.

(d) **Complete the petty cash reimbursement document below to restore the imprest amount of £120.**

Petty cash reimbursement		
Date: 31.07.20XX		
Amount required to restore the cash in the petty cash box	£	

Hazelcombe & Co maintains a petty cash book as a book of prime entry only. The following transactions all took place on 30 June and have been entered in the petty cash book as shown below. No entries have yet been made in the general ledger.

Petty cash book – credit side

Date 20XX	Details	Amount £	VAT £	Distribution expenses £	Travel £	Office expenses £
30 Jun	Envelopes	18.24	3.04			15.20
30 Jun	Postage	13.40				13.40
30 Jun	De-icer	6.72	1.12	5.60		
30 Jun	Bus fares	17.65			17.65	
		56.01	4.16	5.60	17.65	28.60

(e) **What will be the FIVE entries in the general ledger?**

General ledger

Account name	Amount £	Debit ✓	Credit ✓
▼			
▼			
▼			
▼			
▼			

Picklist:

Bank
Bus fares
De-icer
Distribution expenses
Envelopes
Office expenses
Petty cash control
Postage
Travel
VAT

Task 6

Below is a list of balances to be transferred to the trial balance as at 30 June.

Place the figures in the debit or credit column, as appropriate, and total each column. Do not enter figures with decimal places in this task and do not enter a zero in the empty column.

Account name	Amount £	Debit £	Credit £
Advertising	789		
Bank (overdraft)	2,137		
Capital	5,000		
Commission income	1,356		
Discounts allowed	1,986		
Discounts received	2,543		
Distribution expenses	9,110		
Furniture and fittings	18,750		
Inventory	12,354		
Loan from bank	10,000		
Maintenance	1,035		
Office expenses	13,728		
Petty cash	250		
Purchases	66,390		
Purchases ledger control	6,297		
Purchases returns	3,287		
Rent and rates	8,265		
Sales	172,242		
Sales ledger control	24,910		
Sales returns	2,890		
Telephone and internet	2,165		
Travel	1,023		
VAT (owing to HM Revenue & Customs)	5,320		
Wages and salaries	44,537		
Totals			

Task 7

A supply of parts has been delivered to Hazelcombe & Co by Handiparts Ltd. The purchase order sent from Hazelcombe & Co, and the invoice from Handiparts Ltd, are shown below.

Hazelcombe & Co
42 Turnstile Trading Estate
Luscombe
LU9 0FG

Purchase Order No. 89374

To: Handiparts Ltd

Date: 10 July 20XX

Please supply 5000 facings, product code 76253AA
Purchase price: £22.00 per 50, plus VAT
Discount: less 20% trade discount, as agreed

Handiparts Ltd
87 Radley Road, Luscombe LU8 4AZ
VAT Registration No. 874 2309 93

Invoice No. 8749

Hazelcombe & Co
42 Turnstile Trading Estate
Luscombe
LU9 0FG

12 July 20XX

5000 facings product code 7253AA @ £0.50 each	£2,500.00
Less trade discount at 20%	£500.00
Net amount	£2,000.00
VAT @ 20%	£ 400.00
Total	£2,400.00

Terms: 30 days net

(a) **Check the invoice against the purchase order and answer the following questions.**

	Yes ✓	No ✓
Has the correct purchase price of the facings been charged?		
Has the correct discount rate been applied?		
What would be the VAT amount charged if the invoice was correct?	£	
What would be the total amount charged if the invoice was correct?	£	

Shown below is a statement of account received from a credit supplier, SpareParts plc, and the supplier's account as shown in the purchases ledger of Hazelcombe & Co.

SpareParts plc Unit 50 Hunston Park Trading Estate Luscombe LU3 6XC				
To: Hazelcombe & Co 42 Turnstile Trading Estate Luscombe LU9 0FG				

STATEMENT OF ACCOUNT

Date 20XX	Number	Details	Amount £	Balance £
15 May	1893	Invoice	2,395	2,395
6 June	C043	Credit note	−456	1,939
11 June	1999	Invoice	7,832	9,771
17 June	1034	Invoice	2,347	12,118
30 June		Payment	−2,395	9,723

SpareParts plc

Date 20XX	Details	Amount £	Date 20XX	Details	Amount £
29 June	Bank – cheque	2,395	15 May	Purchases	2,395
29 June	Bank – discount	27	11 June	Purchases	7,832
			17 June	Purchases	2,347

(b) **Which item is missing from the statement of account from SpareParts plc?**

▼

Picklist:

Credit note C043
Invoice I893
Invoice I999
Invoice I034
Cheque for £2,395
Discount for £27

(c) **Which item is missing from the supplier account in Hazelcombe & Co's purchases ledger?**

▼

Picklist:

Credit note C043
Invoice I893
Invoice I999
Invoice I034
Cheque for £2,395
Discount for £27

(d) **Assuming any differences between the statement of account from SpareParts plc and the supplier account in Hazelcombe & Co's purchases ledger are simply due to omission errors, what is the amount owing to SpareParts plc?**

£

Hazelcombe & Co sends out cheques to suppliers on the last Wednesday of the month following the month of the relevant invoice or credit note. Below is an extract from the purchases ledger of Hazelcombe & Co.

Cooper Foundry Ltd

Date 20XX	Details	Amount £	Date 20XX	Details	Amount £
29 May	Purchases returns (credit note 039)	45	25 May	Purchases invoice 09364	982
6 June	Purchases returns (credit note 124)	63	1 June	Purchases invoice 09528	2,386
29 June	Bank	937	19 July	Purchases invoice 09785	1,802

(e) Invoice number 09785 will be paid by Hazelcombe & Co in

	✓
June	
July	
August	
September	

Task 8

On 10 July Hazelcombe & Co delivered the following goods to a credit customer, Warriner plc.

Hazelcombe & Co
42 Turnstile Trading Estate
Luscombe
LU9 0FG

Delivery note No. 90230
10 July 20XX

Warriner plc   Customer account code: W981
45 Printer Lane
Luscombe
LU3 9LA

500 fixings, product code FX827.

The list price of the goods was £20.00 per box of 10 fixings plus VAT. Warriner plc is to be given a 20% trade discount and a 2% early settlement discount.

(a) **Complete the invoice below.**

Hazelcombe & Co
42 Turnstile Trading Estate
Luscombe
LU9 0FG

VAT Registration No. 928 2781 110

Warriner plc   Customer account code: W981
45 Printer Lane
Luscombe
LU3 9LA

                                            Date: 11 July 20XX

Invoice No: 21026
Delivery note number: 90230

Quantity of goods	Product code	Total list price £	Net amount after trade discount £	VAT £	Gross £

Hazelcombe & Co offers each customer a discount of 5% if any order amounts to £2,000 or over.

(b) **What is the name of this type of discount?**

▼

Picklist:

Bulk discount
Settlement discount
Trade discount

The account shown below is in the sales ledger of Hazelcombe & Co. A remittance advice for an automated payment of £1,534 has now been received from this customer.

Oster Ltd

Date 20XX	Details	Amount £	Date 20XX	Details	Amount £
15 May	Sales invoice 19011	1,920	28 May	Sales returns credit note 801	84
16 June	Sales invoice 20332	1,743	15 June	Bank	1,836
17 July	Sales invoice 21276	1,633	21 June	Sales returns credit note 893	209

(c) **Which outstanding item has not been included in the payment of £1,534?**

▼

Picklist:

Sales invoice 19011
Sales invoice 20332
Sales invoice 21276
Bank
Sales returns credit note 801
Sales returns credit note 893

An invoice is being prepared to be sent Oster Ltd for £1,180.00 plus VAT of £231.28. A settlement discount of 2% will be offered for payment within 10 days.

(d) **What is the amount Hazelcombe & Co should receive if payment is made within 10 days?**

£

(e) **What is the amount Hazelcombe & Co should receive if payment is NOT made within 10 days?**

£

Task 9

The following two accounts are in the general ledger at the close of day on 30 June.

(a) **Insert the balance carried down together with date and details.**
(b) **Insert the totals.**
(c) **Insert the balance brought down together with date and details.**

Office expenses

Date 20XX	Details	Amount £	Date 20XX	Details	Amount £
01 Jun	Balance b/d	12,945		▼	
30 Jun	Petty cash	42		▼	
30 Jun	Purchases ledger control	523		▼	
	▼			▼	
	Total			Total	
	▼			▼	

Picklist:

Balance b/d
Balance c/d
Bank
Petty cash
Purchases ledger control

Commission received

Date 20XX	Details	Amount £	Date 20XX	Details	Amount £
	▼		01 Jun	Balance b/d	1,276
	▼		30 Jun	Bank	18
	▼			▼	
	Total			Total	
	▼			▼	

Picklist:

Balance b/d
Balance c/d
Bank
Petty cash
Sales ledger control

The following is a summary of transactions with Tarsus & Co, a new credit customer.

£1,430 re invoice 21104 of 13 July
£213 re credit note 920 of 17 July
£947 re invoice 21309 of 22 July
Cheque for £1,020 received 30 July
Settlement discount £15 taken 30 July

(d) **Complete the statement of account below.**

Hazelcombe & Co
42 Turnstile Trading Estate
Luscombe
LU9 0FG

To: Tarsus & Co   Date: 31 July 20XX

Date 20XX	Details	Transaction amount £	Outstanding amount £
13 July	Invoice 21104		
17 July	Credit note 920		
22 July	Invoice 21309		
30 July	Cheque		
30 July	Discount taken		

Task 10

It is important to understand the difference between capital expenditure, revenue expenditure, capital income and revenue income.

(a) **Select one option in each instance below to show whether the item will be capital expenditure, revenue expenditure, capital income or revenue income.**

Item	Capital expenditure ✓	Revenue expenditure ✓	Capital income ✓	Revenue income ✓
Cash sales				
Purchase on credit of lights for resale				
Sale of goods on credit				
Purchase of office computer				
Payments to credit suppliers				
Receipt from sale of an item of Hazelcombe & Co's furniture and fittings				

(b) **Show whether the following statements are True or False.**

	True ✓	False ✓
An increase in an asset is shown as a credit entry in the general ledger		
A decrease in liabilities is shown as a credit entry in the general ledger		
An increase in capital is shown as a credit entry in the general ledger		

(c) **Identify from the picklist an example of an asset, a liability and a capital transaction.**

Item	Example from picklist
Asset	▼
Liability	▼
Capital transaction	▼

Picklist:

Trade receivables
Bank overdraft
Drawings

BPP PRACTICE ASSESSMENT 2
PROCESSING BOOKKEEPING
TRANSACTIONS

ANSWERS

Processing Bookkeeping Transactions BPP practice assessment 2

Task 1

(a) – (b)

Purchases returns day book

Date 20XX	Details	Credit note number	Total £	VAT £	Net £	Purchases returns £
30 Jun	Sindar Ltd	CN873	2,112	352	1,760	1,760
30 Jun	Premier Inc	02936	2,496	416	2,080	2,080
30 Jun	Bargain Parts plc	1092/22	144	24	120	120
	Totals		4,752	792	3,960	3,960

(c)

Supplier code	F920
General ledger code	GL971

(d) The correct answer is: to help identify the amount spent on a particular category of inventory

Task 2

(a)

Purchases ledger

Account name	Amount £	Debit ✓	Credit ✓
Lindemann plc	5,328		✓
Stoke Rows Ltd	3,840		✓
Foster Brothers	1,536		✓
Osman Ltd	2,688		✓

(b)

General ledger

Account name	Amount £	Debit ✓	Credit ✓
Purchases	11,160	✓	
Purchases ledger control	13,392		✓
VAT	2,232	✓	

(c)

Sales ledger

Account name	Amount £	Debit ✓	Credit ✓
Tristram Steers & Co	2,832		✓
Austen Knight plc	144		✓

(d)

General ledger

Account name	Amount £	Debit ✓	Credit ✓
Sales ledger control	2,976		✓
Sales returns	2,480	✓	
VAT	496	✓	

Task 3

(a)

Cash book – credit side

Details	Discount £	Cash £	Bank £	VAT £	Trade payables £	Cash purchases £	Maintenance £
Balance b/f			1,902				
Wisper & Co		1,104		184		920	
Forback Ltd		192		32		160	
Cresswell plc		193				193	
Lampetus Ltd	25		2,135		2,135		
GMG Maintenance Services			426	71			355
Total	25	1,489	4,463	287	2,135	1,273	355

(b)

Cash book – debit side

Details	Discount £	Cash £	Bank £	Trade receivables £
Balance b/f		1,593		
Prickles & Co			2,837	2,837
Dreston Proops	75		3,299	3,299
Total	75	1,593	6,136	6,136

(c) The correct answer is: £104 (1,593 – 1,489 = 104)

(d) The correct answer is: £1,673 (6,136 – 4,463 = 1,673)

(e) The correct answer is: Debit

Task 4

(a)

Sales ledger

Account name	Amount £	Debit ✓	Credit ✓
Gwendolin Ltd	643		✓
Gwendolin Ltd	15		✓
Marcham & Co	2,309		✓

(b)

General ledger

General ledger			
Account name	Amount £	Debit ✓	Credit ✓
Sales ledger control	2,952		✓
Sales ledger control	15		✓
Discounts allowed	15	✓	

(c)

Purchases ledger

Account name	Amount £	Debit ✓	Credit ✓
Bradfield & Co	2,385	✓	

(d)

General ledger

Account name	Amount £	Debit ✓	Credit ✓
Purchases ledger control	2,385	✓	
Cash purchases	200	✓	
VAT	40	✓	

Task 5

(a) – (b)

Petty cash book

Debit side		Credit side					
Details	Amount £	Details	Amount £	VAT £	Stationery £	Travel £	Postage £
Balance b/f	120.00	Quick Bus Company	12.50			12.50	
		Star's Stationery	21.60	3.60	18.00		
		Post Office	8.00				8.00
		Balance c/d	77.90				
	120.00		120.00	3.60	18.00	12.50	8.00

(c)

Amount in petty cash box	£	78.34
Balance on petty cash account	£	81.26
Difference	£	2.92

(d)

Petty cash reimbursement		
Date: 31.07.20XX		
Amount required to restore the cash in the petty cash box	£	112.23

(e)

General ledger

Account name	Amount £	Debit ✓	Credit ✓
Petty cash control	56.01		✓
Distribution expenses	5.60	✓	
Office expenses	28.60	✓	
Travel	17.65	✓	
VAT	4.16	✓	

Task 6

Account name	Amount £	Debit £	Credit £
Advertising	789	789	
Bank (overdraft)	2,137		2,137
Capital	5,000		5,000
Commission income	1,356		1,356
Discounts allowed	1,986	1,986	
Discounts received	2,543		2,543
Distribution expenses	9,110	9,110	
Furniture and fittings	18,750	18,750	
Inventory	12,354	12,354	
Loan from bank	10,000		10,000
Maintenance	1,035	1,035	
Office expenses	13,728	13,728	
Petty cash	250	250	
Purchases	66,390	66,390	
Purchases ledger control	6,297		6,297
Purchases returns	3,287		3,287
Rent and rates	8,265	8,265	
Sales	172,242		172,242
Sales ledger control	24,910	24,910	
Sales returns	2,890	2,890	
Telephone and internet	2,165	2,165	
Travel	1,023	1,023	
VAT (owing to HM Revenue & Customs)	5,320		5,320
Wages and salaries	44,537	44,537	
Totals		208,182	208,182

Task 7

(a) VAT: $((5{,}000 \times 22/50) - (5{,}000 \times 22/50 \times 20/100)) \times 20/100 = 352$

Total: $(5{,}000 \times 22/50) \times 0.80 \times 1.2 = 2{,}112$

	Yes ✓	No ✓
Has the correct purchase price of the facings been charged?		✓
Has the correct discount rate been applied?	✓	
What would be the VAT amount charged if the invoice was correct?	£	352
What would be the total amount charged if the invoice was correct?	£	2,112

(b) The correct answer is: discount for £27

(c) The correct answer is: credit note C043

(d) The correct answer is: £9,696

Working

£9,723 – £27 = £9,696

(e) The correct answer is: August

Task 8

(a) VAT: (800 – (800 × 2/100)) × 20/100 = 156.80

<table>
<tr><td colspan="6">Hazelcombe & Co
42 Turnstile Trading Estate
Luscombe
LU9 0FG</td></tr>
<tr><td colspan="6" align="center">VAT Registration No. 928 2781 110</td></tr>
<tr><td colspan="3">Warriner plc
45 Printer Lane
Luscombe
LU3 9LA

Invoice No: 21026
Delivery note number: 90230</td><td colspan="3">Customer account code: W981

Date: 11 July 20XX</td></tr>
<tr>
<td>Quantity of goods</td>
<td>Product code</td>
<td>Total list price

£</td>
<td>Net amount after trade discount

£</td>
<td>VAT

£</td>
<td>Gross

£</td>
</tr>
<tr>
<td>500</td>
<td>FX827</td>
<td>1,000.00</td>
<td>800.00</td>
<td>156.80</td>
<td>956.80</td>
</tr>
</table>

(b) The correct answer is: bulk discount

(c) The correct answer is: sales invoice 21276

(d) The correct answer is: £1,387.68

Working

(£1,180 × 98%) + £231.28 = £1,387.68

(e) The correct answer is: £1,411.28

Working

(1,180.00 + 231.28 = 1,411.28)

....

Task 9

(a) – (c)

Office expenses

Date 20XX	Details	Amount £	Date 20XX	Details	Amount £
01 Jun	Balance b/d	12,945			
30 Jun	Petty cash	42			
30 Jun	Purchases ledger control	523			
			30 Jun	Balance c/d	13,510
	Total	13,510		Total	13,510
1 Jul	Balance b/d	13,510			

Commission received

Date 20XX	Details	Amount £	Date 20XX	Details	Amount £
			01 Jun	Balance b/d	1,276
			30 Jun	Bank	18
30 Jun	Balance c/d	1,294			
	Total	1,294		Total	1,294
			1 Jul	Balance b/d	1,294

(d)

Hazelcombe & Co
42 Turnstile Trading Estate
Luscombe
LU9 0FG

To: Tarsus & Co   Date: 31 July 20XX

Date 20XX	Details	Transaction amount £	Outstanding amount £
13 July	Invoice 21104	1,430	1,430
17 July	Credit note 920	213	1,217
22 July	Invoice 21309	947	2,164
30 July	Cheque	1,020	1,144
30 July	Discount taken	15	1,129

Task 10

(a)

Item	Capital expenditure ✓	Revenue expenditure ✓	Capital income ✓	Revenue income ✓
Cash sales				✓
Purchase on credit of lights for resale		✓		
Sale of goods on credit				✓
Purchase of office computer	✓			
Payments to credit suppliers		✓		
Receipt from sale of an item of Hazelcombe & Co's furniture and fittings			✓	

(b)

	True ✓	False ✓
An increase in an asset is shown as a credit entry in the general ledger		✓
A decrease in liabilities is shown as a credit entry in the general ledger		✓
An increase in capital is shown as a credit entry in the general ledger	✓	

(c)

Item	Example
Asset	Trade receivables
Liability	Bank overdraft
Capital transaction	Drawings

BPP PRACTICE ASSESSMENT 3
PROCESSING BOOKKEEPING
TRANSACTIONS

Time allowed: 2 hours

Processing Bookkeeping Transactions BPP practice assessment 3

All answers should be rounded to the nearest penny unless otherwise instructed.

Task 1

Invoices from suppliers have been checked and partially entered in the purchases day book, as shown below.

(a) **Complete the entries in the purchases day book by inserting the appropriate figures for each invoice.**

(b) **Total the last five columns of the purchases day book.**

Purchases day book

Date 20XX	Details	Invoice number	Total £	VAT £	Net £	Women's clothing £	Men's clothing £
30 Jun	Forfar Textiles plc	C9230	1,872				1,560
30 Jun	Jessamy Fashion Inc	0024567	3,216		2,680	2,680	
30 Jun	Lindstrom Ltd	726		648		3,240	
	Totals						

Mandarin Ltd codes all purchase invoices with a supplier code AND a general ledger code. A selection of the codes used is given below.

Supplier	Supplier Code
Dapple Ltd	PL189
Gadabout UK plc	PL394
Indigo & Co	PL522
New Aim Ltd	PL703
Roughtrap Ltd	PL947

Item	General Ledger Code
Men's shirts	GL001
Men's trousers	GL002
Women's tops	GL003
Women's trousers	GL004
Sundry clothing	GL005

This is an invoice received from a supplier.

New Aim Ltd
35 Didcot Road, Cinnadon CN7 3DD
VAT Registration No. 356 2368 302

Mandarin Ltd
Mandarin House
25 Jedward Street
Cinnadon
CN6 6LW

23 July 20XX

30 womens trousers (product code WT673) @ £16 each	£480.00
VAT @ 20%	£96.00
Total	£576.00

(c) **Select which codes would be used to code this invoice.**

Supplier code	▼
General ledger code	▼

Picklist:

GL001
GL002
GL003
GL004
GL005
PL189
PL394
PL522
PL703
PL947

(d) In order to identify how much is owed to a supplier at any point in time, purchases invoices are coded with a

Picklist:

General ledger code
Supplier code
Customer code
Product code

Task 2

The following transactions all took place on 30 June and have been entered into the sales day book as shown below. No entries have yet been made into the ledger system.

Sales day book

Date 20XX	Details	Invoice number	Total £	VAT £	Net £
30 Jun	Trencher plc	3452	672	112	560
30 Jun	Simons and Daughters	3453	1,968	328	1,640
30 Jun	Coker Ltd	3454	864	144	720
30 Jun	Marchmain & Co	3455	3,024	504	2,520
	Totals		6,528	1,088	5,440

(a) **What will be the entries in the sales ledger?**

Sales ledger

Account name	Amount £	Debit ✓	Credit ✓
▼			
▼			
▼			
▼			

Picklist:

Coker Ltd
Marchmain & Co
Purchases
Purchases ledger control
Purchases returns
Sales
Sales ledger control
Sales returns
Simons and Daughters
Trencher plc
VAT

(b) **What will be the entries in the general ledger?**

General ledger

Account name	Amount £	Debit ✓	Credit ✓
▼			
▼			
▼			

Picklist:

Coker Ltd
Marchmain & Co
Purchases
Purchases ledger control
Purchases returns
Sales
Sales ledger control
Sales returns
Simons and Daughters
Trencher plc
VAT

The following credit transactions all took place on 30 June and have been entered into the purchases returns day book as shown below. No entries have yet been made in the ledgers.

Purchases returns day book

Date 20XX	Details	Credit note number	Total £	VAT £	Net £
30 June	Bester plc	0923	96	16	80
30 June	Newsome Ltd	C6478	432	72	360
	Totals		528	88	440

(c) **What will be the entries in the purchases ledger?**

Purchases ledger

Account name	Amount £	Debit ✓	Credit ✓
▼			
▼			

Picklist:

Bester plc
Newsome Ltd
Purchases
Purchases ledger control
Purchases returns
Sales
Sales ledger control
Sales returns
VAT

(d) **What will be the entries in the general ledger?**

General ledger

Account name	Amount £	Debit ✓	Credit ✓
▼			
▼			
▼			

Picklist:

Bester plc
Newsome Ltd
Purchases
Purchases ledger control
Purchases returns
Sales
Sales ledger control
Sales returns
VAT

Task 3

Scriven Trading has made five payments which are to be entered in its cash book.

Receipts for payments

Received cash with thanks for goods bought. From Scriven Trading, a customer without a credit account. Net £640 VAT £128 Total £768 *Amdegus Ltd*	Received cash with thanks for goods bought. From Scriven Trading, a customer without a credit account. Net £265 VAT £53 Total £318 *Strenta Co*	Received cash with thanks for goods bought. From Scriven Trading, a customer without a credit account. Net £501 (No VAT) *Banrix & Sons*

Cheque book counterfoils

Diston Ltd (Purchases ledger account DIS057) £4,295 (Note: Have taken £33 settlement discount) 209345	Opra Office Supplies (We have no credit account with this supplier) £336 including VAT 209346

(a) **Enter the details from the three receipts and two cheque book stubs into the credit side of the cash book shown below and total each column.**

Cash book – credit side

Details	Discount £	Cash £	Bank £	VAT £	Trade payables £	Cash purchases £	Office expenses £
Balance b/f			1,249				
Amdegus Ltd							
Strenta Co							
Banrix & Sons							
Diston Ltd							
Opra Office Supplies							
Total							

There are also two cheques from credit customers to be entered in Scriven Trading's cash book:

Vampeter Ltd	£1,256
Propos Co	£8,903 (this customer has taken a £100 discount)

(b) **Enter the above details into the debit side of the cash book and total each column.**

Cash book – debit side

Details	Discount £	Cash £	Bank £	Trade receivables £
Balance b/f		1,869		
Vampeter Ltd				
Propos Co				
Total				

(c) **Using your answers to (a) and (b) above, calculate the cash balance.**

£

(d) **Using your answers to (a) and (b) above, calculate the bank balance.**

£

(e) **Will the bank balance calculated in (d) above be a debit or credit balance?**

	✓
Debit	
Credit	

Task 4

The following transactions all took place on 30 June and have been entered in the debit side of the cash book as shown below. No entries have yet been made in the ledgers.

Cash book – debit side

Date 20XX	Details	Cash £	Bank £	VAT £	Trade receivables £	Cash sales £
30 Jun	Singer & Co		1,934		1,934	
30 Jun	Cash sale	756		126		630

(a) **What will be the entry in the sales ledger?**

Sales ledger

Account name	Amount £	Debit ✓	Credit ✓
▼			

Picklist:

Bank
Cash
Cash sales
Discounts allowed
Discounts received
Purchases
Purchases ledger control
Sales
Sales ledger control
Singer & Co
VAT

(b) **What will be the THREE entries in the general ledger?**

General ledger

Account name	Amount £	Debit ✓	Credit ✓
▼			
▼			
▼			

Picklist:

Bank
Cash
Cash sales
Discounts allowed
Discounts received
Purchases
Purchases ledger control
Sales
Sales ledger control
Singer & Co
VAT

The following transactions took place on 30 June and have been entered in the credit side of the cash book as shown below. No entries have yet been made in the ledgers.

Cash book – credit side

Date 20XX	Details	Discount £	Bank £
30 Jun	Balance b/d		966
30 Jun	Vincent plc	121	2,377

(c) **What will be the THREE entries in the general ledger?**

General ledger

Account name	Amount £	Debit ✓	Credit ✓
▼			
▼			
▼			

Picklist:

Bank
Discounts allowed
Discounts received
Purchases
Purchases ledger control
Sales
Sales ledger control
VAT
Vincent plc

Task 5

This is a summary of petty cash payments made by Scriven Trading.

Post office paid	£8.70 (no VAT)
Harry's Café paid	£26.30 (no VAT)
Tune Travel paid	£32.40 (plus VAT)

(a) **Enter the above transactions, in the order in which they are shown, in the petty cash book below.**

(b) **Total the petty cash book and show the balance carried down.**

Petty cash book

Debit side		Credit side					
Details	Amount £	Details	Amount £	VAT £	Entertainment £	Travel £	Postage £
Balance b/f	180.00	▼					
		▼					
		▼					
		▼					
		▼					

Picklist:

Amount
Balance b/d
Balance c/d
Details
Entertainment
Harry's Café
Postage
Post Office
Travel
Tune Travel
VAT

Part way through the month the petty cash account had a balance of £73.17. The cash in the petty cash box was checked and the following notes and coins were there.

Notes and coins	£
2 × £20 notes	40.00
2 × £10 notes	20.00
1 × £5 notes	5.00
2 × £2 coins	4.00
2 × £1 coins	2.00
0 × 50p coins	0.00
1 × 10p coins	0.10
1 × 5p coins	0.05
7 × 1p coins	0.07

(c) **Reconcile the cash amount in the petty cash box with the balance on the petty cash account.**

Amount in petty cash box	£	
Balance on petty cash account	£	
Difference	£	

At the end of the month the cash in the petty cash box was £8.53.

(d) **Complete the petty cash reimbursement document below to restore the imprest amount of £180.**

Petty cash reimbursement		
Date: 31.07.20XX		
Amount required to restore the cash in the petty cash box	£	

Mandarin Ltd maintains a petty cash book as a book of prime entry only. The following transactions all took place on 30 June and have been entered in the petty cash book (credit side) as shown below. No entries have yet been made in the general ledger.

Petty cash book – credit side

Date 20XX	Details	Amount £	VAT £	Motor expenses £	Postage £	Sundry expenses £
30 Jun	Taxi fares	15.98				15.98
30 Jun	Printer paper	8.16	1.36			6.80
30 Jun	Petrol	51.36	8.56	42.80		
30 Jun	Postage stamps	17.26			17.26	
		92.76	9.92	42.80	17.26	22.78

(e) **What will be the FIVE entries in the general ledger?**

General ledger

Account name		Amount £	Debit ✓	Credit ✓
	▼			
	▼			
	▼			
	▼			
	▼			

Picklist:

Bank
Motor expenses
Sundry expenses
Petrol
Petty cash control
Postage
Postage stamps
Printer paper
Taxi fares
VAT

Task 6

Below is a list of balances to be transferred to the trial balance as at 30 June.

Place the figures in the debit or credit column, as appropriate, and total each column. Do not enter figures with decimal places in this task and do not enter a zero in the empty column.

Account name	Amount £	Debit £	Credit £
Marketing	2,534		
Cash at bank	9,267		
Capital	10,000		
Heat and light	3,289		
Discounts allowed	1,004		
Discounts received	2,940		
Motor expenses	3,098		
Motor vehicles	15,000		
Loan from bank	12,500		
Administration expenses	5,903		
Insurance	498		
Petty cash	100		
Purchases	89,262		
Purchases ledger control	7,438		
Purchases returns	2,907		
Premises costs	5,097		
Sales	166,242		
Sales ledger control	11,892		
Sales returns	3,022		
Inventory	16,006		
Training expenses	2,786		
Travel	457		
VAT (owing to HM Revenue & Customs)	2,455		
Salaries	35,267		
Totals			

Task 7

A supply of clothing has been delivered to Mandarin Ltd by Rainbow Fashions Ltd. The purchase order sent from Mandarin Ltd, and the invoice from Rainbow Fashions Ltd, are shown below.

Mandarin Ltd
Mandarin House, 25 Jedward Street
Cinnadon
CN6 6LW

Purchase Order No. 093247

To: Rainbow Fashions Ltd

Date: 17 July 20XX

Please supply 40 mens polo shirts, product code MPS45
Purchase price: £36 00 per pack of 5, plus VAT
Discount: less 10% trade discount, as agreed

Rainbow Fashions Ltd
92 Norman Street, Cinnadon CN4 2KJ
VAT Registration No. 903 2838 39

Invoice No. 83792

Mandarin Ltd
Mandarin House, 25 Jedward Street
Cinnadon
CN6 6LW

22 July 20XX

40 mens polo shirts product code MPS45 @ £7.60 each	£304.00
Less trade discount at 10%	£30.40
Net amount	£273.60
VAT @ 20%	£54.72
Total	£328.32

Terms: 30 days net

(a) **Check the invoice against the purchase order and answer the following questions.**

	Yes ✓	No ✓
Has the correct purchase price of the polo shirts been charged?		
Has the correct discount been applied?		
What would be the VAT amount charged if the invoice was correct?	£	
What would be the total amount charged if the invoice was correct?	£	

Shown below is a statement of account received from a credit supplier, and the supplier's account as shown in the purchases ledger of Mandarin Ltd.

Bella Designs
34-36 Bath Street
Cinnadon
CN3 1GH

To: Mandarin Ltd
Mandarin House
25 Jedward Street
Cinnadon
CN6 6LW

STATEMENT OF ACCOUNT

Date 20XX	Number	Details	Amount £	Balance £
26 May	6723	Invoice	1,092	1,092
3 June	6801	Invoice	894	1,986
15 June		Payment	−1,986	0
15 June	7013	Invoice	3,267	3,267
18 June	C67	Credit note	−62	3,205
27 Jun	7226	Invoice	2,674	5,879
30 June	C98	Credit note	−89	5,790

Bella Designs

Date 20XX	Details	Amount £	Date 20XX	Details	Amount £
15 June	Bank – cheque	1,986	26 May	Purchases	1,092
18 June	Purchases returns	62	3 June	Purchases	894
30 June	Bank – cheque	3,205	15 June	Purchases	3,267
			27 June	Purchases	2,674

(b) **Which item is missing from the statement of account from Bella Designs?**

▼

Picklist:

Credit note C67
Credit note C98
Invoice 6723
Invoice 6801
Invoice 7013
Invoice 7226
Payment for £1,986
Payment for £3,205

(c) **Which item is missing from the supplier account in Mandarin Ltd's purchases ledger?**

▼

Picklist:

Credit note C67
Credit note C98
Invoice 6723
Invoice 6801
Invoice 7013
Invoice 7226
Payment for £1,986
Payment for £3,205

(d) **Assuming any differences between the statement of account from Bella Designs and the supplier account in Mandarin Ltd's purchases ledger are simply due to omission errors, what is the amount owing to Bella Designs?**

£

Mandarin Ltd sends out remittance advice notes with cheques to suppliers on the last working day of the month following the month of the relevant invoice or credit note.

(e) **Which of the following statements is True?**

	✓
The remittance advice note is a book of prime entry	
The remittance advice note is part of the general ledger	
The remittance advice note is part of the purchases ledger	
The remittance advice note is sent to the supplier	

Task 8

On 21 July Mandarin Ltd delivered the following goods to a credit customer, Jessop Brothers.

Mandarin Ltd
Mandarin House
25 Jedward Street
Cinnadon
CN6 6LW

Delivery note No. 452634
21 July 20XX

Jessop Brothers   Customer account code: SL930
Unit 10 Eastern Trading Estate
Cinnadon
CN1 1PP

720 womens decorative tops, product code WT555.

The list price of the goods was £30 per box of six tops plus VAT. Jessop Brothers is to be given a 10% bulk discount and a 5% early settlement discount.

(a) **Complete the invoice below.**

Mandarin Ltd
Mandarin House, 25 Jedward Street
Cinnadon
CN6 6LW

VAT Registration No. 928 2781 110

Jessop Brothers   Customer account code: SL930
Unit 10 Eastern Trading Estate
Cinnadon
CN1 1PP

Date: 22 July 20XX
Invoice No:01256
Delivery note number: 452634

Quantity of goods	Product code	Total list price £	Net amount after bulk discount £	VAT £	Gross £

Mandarin Ltd offers some established customers a discount of 5% whatever the size of their order and irrespective of when they pay.

(b) **What is the name of this type of discount?**

▼

Picklist:

Bulk discount
Settlement discount
Trade discount

Task 9

The following two accounts are in the general ledger at the close of day on 30 June.

(a) **Insert the balance carried down together with date and details.**
(b) **Insert the totals.**
(c) **Insert the balance brought down together with date and details.**

Motor expenses

Date 20XX	Details	Amount £	Date 20XX	Details	Amount £
01 Jun	Balance b/d	2,904		▼	
15 Jun	Purchases ledger control	276		▼	
30 Jun	Purchases ledger control	184		▼	
	▼			▼	
	Total			Total	
	▼			▼	

Picklist:

Balance b/d
Balance c/d
Bank
Purchases ledger control
Sales ledger control

Discounts received

Date 20XX	Details	Amount £	Date 20XX	Details	Amount £
	▼		01 Jun	Balance b/d	926
	▼		15 Jun	Purchases ledger control	64
	▼		30 Jun	Purchases ledger control	25
	▼			▼	
	Total			Total	
	▼			▼	

Picklist:

Balance b/d
Balance c/d
Bank
Purchases ledger control
Sales ledger control

The following is a summary of transactions with Tarsus & Co, a new credit customer.

£324 re invoice 01250 of 21 July
£12 re credit note 013 of 22 July
£1,285 re invoice 01301 of 30 July
Cheque for £302 received 31 July
Settlement discount £10 taken 31 July

(d)   **Complete the statement of account below.**

Mandarin Ltd
Mandarin House
25 Jedward Street
Cinnadon
CN6 6LW

To: Tarsus & Co   Date: 31 July 20XX

Date 20XX	Details	Transaction amount £	Outstanding amount £
21 July	Invoice 01250		
22 July	Credit note 013		
30 July	Invoice 01301		
31 July	Cheque		
31 July	Discount taken		

The account shown below is in the sales ledger of Mandarin Ltd. A remittance advice for an automated payment of £1,565 has now been received from this customer.

Plews & Co

Date 20XX	Details	Amount £	Date 20XX	Details	Amount £
12 May	Sales invoice 0024	2,910	15 May	Sales returns credit note 001	125
23 June	Sales invoice 0095	1,663	25 June	Sales returns credit note 017	98
2 July	Sales invoice 0102	2,739	30 June	Bank	2,785

(e) **Which outstanding item has not been included in the payment of £1,565?**

Picklist:

Sales invoice 0024
Sales invoice 0095
Sales invoice 0102
Bank
Sales returns credit note 001
Sales returns credit note 017

An invoice is being prepared to be sent to Plews & Co for £2,560.00 plus VAT of £486.40. A settlement discount of 5% will be offered for payment within 10 days.

(f) **What is the amount Mandarin Ltd should receive if payment is made within 10 days?**

£

(g) **What is the amount Mandarin Ltd should receive if payment is NOT made within 10 days?**

£

Task 10

It is important to understand the difference between capital expenditure, revenue expenditure, capital income and revenue income.

(a) **Select one option in each instance below to show whether the item will be capital expenditure, revenue expenditure, capital income or revenue income.**

Item	Capital expenditure ✓	Revenue expenditure ✓	Capital income ✓	Revenue income ✓
Receipt from sale of a motor vehicle				
Purchase on credit of clothing for resale				
Sale of clothing with one month to pay				
Purchase of shop fittings				
Sale in the factory shop with payment by debit card				
Payment to supplier with one month credit taken				

(b) **Show whether the following statements are True or False.**

	True ✓	False ✓
In a cash transaction the primary documentation is a (till) receipt		
Output tax is the VAT suffered on purchases		
Every three months every business must pay value added tax to HMRC		

(c) **For each of the items below, identify an example from the picklist provided.**

Item	Example
Asset	▼
Liability	▼
Capital transaction	▼

Picklist:

Trade payables
Contribution from owners
Petty cash

BPP PRACTICE ASSESSMENT 3
PROCESSING BOOKKEEPING
TRANSACTIONS

ANSWERS

Processing Bookkeeping Transactions BPP practice assessment 3

Task 1

(a) – (b)

Purchases day book

Date 20XX	Details	Invoice number	Total £	VAT £	Net £	Women's clothing £	Men's clothing £
30 Jun	Forfar Textiles plc	C9230	1,872	312	1,560		1,560
30 Jun	Jessamy Fashion Inc	0024567	3,216	536	2,680	2,680	
30 Jun	Lindstrom Ltd	726	3,888	648	3,240	3,240	
	Totals		8,976	1,496	7,480	5,920	1,560

(c)

Supplier code	PL703
General ledger code	GL004

(d)   The correct answer is: supplier code

....

Task 2

(a)

Sales ledger

Account name	Amount £	Debit ✓	Credit ✓
Trencher plc	672	✓	
Simons and Daughters	1,968	✓	
Coker Ltd	864	✓	
Marchmain & Co	3,024	✓	

(b)

General ledger

Account name	Amount £	Debit ✓	Credit ✓
Sales	5,440		✓
Sales ledger control	6,528	✓	
VAT	1,088		✓

(c)

Purchases ledger

Account name	Amount £	Debit ✓	Credit ✓
Bester plc	96	✓	
Newsome Ltd	432	✓	

(d)

General ledger

Account name	Amount £	Debit ✓	Credit ✓
Purchases ledger control	528	✓	
Purchases returns	440		✓
VAT	88		✓

Task 3

(a) Cash book – credit side

Details	Discount £	Cash £	Bank £	VAT £	Trade payables £	Cash purchases £	Office expenses £
Balance b/f			1,249				
Amdegus Ltd		768		128		640	
Strenta Co		318		53		265	
Banrix & Sons		501				501	
Diston Ltd	33		4,295		4,295		
Opra Office Supplies			336	56			280
Total	33	1,587	5,880	237	4,295	1,406	280

(b) Cash book – debit side

Details	Discount £	Cash £	Bank £	Trade receivables £
Balance b/f		1,869		
Vampeter Ltd			1,256	1,256
Propos Co	100		8,903	8,903
Total	100	1,869	10,159	10,159

(c) The correct answer is: £282 (1,869 – 1,587 = 282)

(d) The correct answer is: £4,279 (10,159 – 5,880 = 4,279)

(e) The correct answer is: Debit

Task 4

(a)

Sales ledger

Account name	Amount £	Debit ✓	Credit ✓
Singer & Co	1,934		✓

(b)

General ledger

Account name	Amount £	Debit ✓	Credit ✓
Sales ledger control	1,934		✓
Cash sales	630		✓
VAT	126		✓

(c)

General ledger

Account name	Amount £	Debit ✓	Credit ✓
Purchases ledger control	2,377	✓	
Purchases ledger control	121	✓	
Discount received	121		✓

Task 5

(a) – (b)

Petty cash book

Debit side		Credit side					
Details	Amount £	Details	Amount £	VAT £	Entertainment £	Travel £	Postage £
Balance b/f	180.00	Post Office	8.70				8.70
		Harry's Café	26.30		26.30		
		Tune Travel	38.88	6.48		32.40	
		Balance c/d	106.12				
	180.00		180.00	6.48	26.30	32.40	8.70

(c)

Amount in petty cash box	£	71.22
Balance on petty cash account	£	73.17
Difference	£	1.95

(d)

Petty cash reimbursement		
Date: 31.07.20XX		
Amount required to restore the cash in the petty cash box	£	171.47

(e)

General ledger

Account name	Amount £	Debit ✓	Credit ✓
Petty cash control	92.76		✓
Motor expenses	42.80	✓	
Sundry expenses	22.78	✓	
Postage	17.26	✓	
VAT	9.92	✓	

Task 6

Account name	Amount £	Debit £	Credit £
Marketing	2,534	2,534	
Cash at bank	9,267	9,267	
Capital	10,000		10,000
Heat and light	3,289	3,289	
Discounts allowed	1,004	1,004	
Discounts received	2,940		2,940
Motor expenses	3,098	3,098	
Motor vehicles	15,000	15,000	
Loan from bank	12,500		12,500
Administration expenses	5,903	5,903	
Insurance	498	498	
Petty cash	100	100	
Purchases	89,262	89,262	
Purchases ledger control	7,438		7,438
Purchases returns	2,907		2,907
Premises costs	5,097	5,097	
Sales	166,242		166,242
Sales ledger control	11,892	11,892	
Sales returns	3,022	3,022	
Inventory	16,006	16,006	
Training expenses	2,786	2,786	
Travel	457	457	
VAT (owing to HM Revenue & Customs)	2,455		2,455
Salaries	35,267	35,267	
Totals		204,482	204,482

Task 7

(a) VAT: ((40 × 36/5) – (40 × 36/5 × 10/100)) × 20/100 = 51.84

Total: ((40 × 36/5) – (40 × 36/5 × 10/100)) × 120/100 = 311.04

	Yes ✓	No ✓
Has the correct purchase price of the polo shirts been charged?		✓
Has the correct discount been applied?	✓	
What would be the VAT amount charged if the invoice was correct?	£	51.84
What would be the total amount charged if the invoice was correct?	£	311.04

(b) The correct answer is: payment for £3,205

(c) The correct answer is: credit note C98

(d) The correct answer is: £2,585

Working

£5,790 – £3,205 = £2,585

(e) The correct answer is: the remittance advice note is sent to the supplier

Task 8

(a)

Mandarin Ltd					
Mandarin House, 25 Jedward Street Cinnadon CN6 6LW					
VAT Registration No. 928 2781 110					
Jessop Brothers Unit 10 Eastern Trading Estate Cinnadon CN1 1PP			Customer account code: SL930		
Invoice No:01256 Delivery note number: 452634			Date: 22 July 20XX		
Quantity of goods	Product code	Total list price £	Net amount after bulk discount £	VAT £	Gross £
720	WT555	3,600.00	3,240.00	615.60	3,855.60

(b)   The correct answer is: trade discount

Task 9

(a) – (c)

Motor expenses

Date 20XX	Details	Amount £	Date 20XX	Details	Amount £
01 Jun	Balance b/d	2,904			
15 Jun	Purchases ledger control	276			
30 Jun	Purchases ledger control	184			
			30 Jun	Balance c/d	3,364
	Total	3,364		Total	3,364
1 Jul	Balance b/d	3,364			

Discounts received

Date 20XX	Details	Amount £	Date 20XX	Details	Amount £
			01 Jun	Balance b/d	926
			15 Jun	PLCA	64
			30 Jun	PLCA	25
30 Jun	Balance c/d	1,015			
	Total	1,015		Total	1,015
			1 Jul	Balance b/d	1,015

(d)

Mandarin Ltd Mandarin House 25 Jedward Street Cinnadon CN6 6LW			
To: Tarsus & Co		Date: 31 July 20XX	
Date 20XX	Details	Transaction amount £	Outstanding amount £
21 July	Invoice 01250	324	324
22 July	Credit note 013	−12	312
30 July	Invoice 01301	1,285	1,597
31 July	Cheque	−302	1,295
31 July	Discount taken	−10	1,285

(e) The correct answer is: sales invoice 0102

(f) The correct answer is: £2,918.40

Working

(£2,560.00 × 95%) + £486.40 = £2,918.40

(g) The correct answer is: £3,046.40

Working

£2,560.00 + £486.40 = £3,046.40

Task 10

(a)

Item	Capital expenditure ✓	Revenue expenditure ✓	Capital income ✓	Revenue income ✓
Receipt from sale of a motor vehicle			✓	
Purchase on credit of clothing for resale		✓		
Sale of clothing with one month to pay				✓
Purchase of shop fittings	✓			
Sale in the factory shop with payment by debit card				✓
Payment to suppliers with one month credit taken		✓		

(b)

	True ✓	False ✓
In a cash transaction the primary documentation is a (till) receipt	✓	
Output tax is the VAT suffered on purchases		✓
Every three months every business must pay value added tax (VAT) to HMRC		✓

(c)

Item	Example
Asset	Petty cash
Liability	Trade payables
Capital transaction	Contribution from owners

BPP PRACTICE ASSESSMENT 4
PROCESSING BOOKKEEPING
TRANSACTIONS

Time allowed: 2 hours

Processing Bookkeeping Transactions BPP practice assessment 4

Task 1

Credit notes to customers have been prepared and partially entered in the sales returns day book, as shown below.

(a) **Complete the entries in the sales returns day book by inserting the appropriate figures for each credit note.**

(b) **Total the last five columns of the sales returns day book.**

Sales returns day book

Date 20XX	Details	Credit note number	Total £	VAT @ 20% £	Net £	Bags returns £	Suitcases returns £
30 Nov	Shrier Goods	562		104		520	
30 Nov	Gringles Co	563	408				340
30 Nov	Lester plc	564	1,068		890	890	
	Totals						

Sumberton Ltd codes all purchase invoices with a supplier code AND a general ledger code. A selection of the codes used is given below.

Supplier	Supplier Code
Casaubon's	PL012
Frankie's Leatherware	PL128
Jane Peel Ltd	PL244
Trinder and Papp	PL301
Wishburton Ltd	PL666

Item	General Ledger Code
Leather bags	GL001
Canvass bags	GL002
Wheeled cases	GL003
Carry cases	GL004
accessories	GL005

This is an invoice received from a supplier.

Jane Peel Ltd
56 Ward End Road, Doristown DO9 3YU
VAT Registration No. 134 1452 22

Sumberton Ltd
Sumberton House
10 Main Road
Sawlow
SA7 5LD

23 December 20XX

10 leather bags (product code R245L) @ £17.50 each	£175.00
VAT @ 20%	£35.00
Total	£210.00

(c) **Select which codes would be used to code this invoice.**

Supplier code	▼
General ledger code	▼

Picklist:

GL001
GL002
GL003
GL004
GL005
PL012
PL128
PL244
PL301
PL666

(d) In order to identify how much has been spent on a particular product for resale at any point in time, purchases invoices are coded with a

▼

Picklist:

General ledger code
Supplier code
Customer code
Product code

Task 2

The following transactions all took place on 30 November and have been entered into the sales day book as shown below. No entries have yet been made into the ledger system.

Sales day book

Date 20XX	Details	Invoice number	Total £	VAT @ 20% £	Net £
30 Nov	Gringles Co	12786	300	50	250
30 Nov	Lester plc	12787	1,308	218	1,090
30 Nov	Shrier Goods	12788	2,676	446	2,230
30 Nov	Abunda Bags	12789	1,992	332	1,660
	Totals		6,276	1,046	5,230

(a) **What will be the entries in the sales ledger?**

Sales ledger

Account name	Amount £	Debit ✓	Credit ✓
▼			
▼			
▼			
▼			

Picklist:

Abunda Bags
Gringles Co
Lester plc
Purchases
Purchases ledger control
Purchases returns
Sales
Sales ledger control
Sales returns
Shrier Goods
VAT

(b) **What will be the entries in the general ledger?**

General ledger

Account name		Amount £	Debit ✓	Credit ✓
	▼			
	▼			
	▼			

Picklist:

Abunda Bags
Gringles Co
Lester plc
Purchases
Purchases ledger control
Purchases returns
Sales
Sales ledger control
Sales returns
Shrier Goods
VAT

The following credit transactions all took place on 30 November and have been entered into the purchases day book as shown below. No entries have yet been made in the ledgers.

Purchases day book

Date 20XX	Details	Invoice number	Total £	VAT @ 20% £	Net £
30 Nov	Frankie's Leatherware	0923	12,348	2,058	10,290
30 Nov	Casaubon's	C6478	3,924	654	3,270
	Totals		16,272	2,712	13,560

(c) **What will be the entries in the purchases ledger?**

Purchases ledger

Account name	Amount £	Debit ✓	Credit ✓
▼			
▼			

Picklist:

Casaubon's
Frankie's Leatherware
Purchases
Purchases ledger control
Purchases returns
Sales
Sales ledger control
Sales returns
VAT

(d) **What will be the entries in the general ledger?**

General ledger

Account name	Amount £	Debit ✓	Credit ✓
▼			
▼			
▼			

Picklist:

Casaubon's
Frankie's Leatherware
Purchases
Purchases ledger control
Purchases returns
Sales
Sales ledger control
Sales returns
VAT

Task 3

There are three receipts to be entered in the debit side of the cash-book during one week.

Cash sales listing

Sale made for cash	Net £	VAT £	Gross £
Humber & Co	485	97	582

Trade receivables listing

Credit customers paying by cheque	Amount paid £	Discounts taken £
Ridgely Ltd	2,150	72
Watts Partners	978	25

(a) **Enter the details from the cash sales listing and the trade receivables listing into the debit side of the cash-book shown below and total each column.**

Cash book – debit side

Details	Discounts £	Cash £	Bank £	VAT £	Trade receivables £	Cash sales £
Balance b/f		159	844			
Humber & Co						
Ridgely Ltd						
Watts Partners						
Total						

Picklist:

Bank
Cash
Cash sales
Discounts
Humber & Co
Ridgely Ltd
Trade receivables
VAT
Watts Partners

The credit side of the cash-book shows cash spent on cash purchases of £561 during the week.

(b) **Using your answer to (a) above, calculate the cash balance.**

£ [   ]

The credit side of the cash-book shows the total amount of cheques sent during the week was £4,085.

(c) **Using your answer to (a) above, calculate the bank balance. If your calculations show that the bank account is overdrawn, your answer should start with a minus sign, for example –123.**

£ [   ]

Task 4

The following transactions all took place on 30 November and have been entered in the credit side of the cash book as shown below. No entries have yet been made in the ledgers.

Cash book – Credit side

Date 20XX	Details	VAT @ 20% £	Bank £
30 Nov	Cash purchase	102	612
30 Nov	Casaubon's		2,445

(a) **What will be the entry in the purchases ledger?**

Purchases ledger

Account name	Amount £	Debit ✓	Credit ✓
▼			

Picklist:

Bank
Casaubon's
Discounts allowed
Discounts received
Purchases
Purchases ledger control
Sales
Sales ledger control
VAT

(b) **What will be the THREE entries in the general ledger?**

General ledger

Account name	Amount £	Debit ✓	Credit ✓
▼			
▼			
▼			

Picklist:

Bank
Casaubon's
Discounts allowed
Discounts received
Purchases
Purchases ledger control
Sales
Sales ledger control
VAT

The following transactions took place on 30 November and have been entered in the debit side of the cash book as shown below. No entries have yet been made in the ledgers.

Cash book – Debit side

Date 20XX	Details	Discount £	Bank £
30 Nov	Balance b/d		3,208
30 Nov	Abunda Bags	56	3,984

(c) **What will be the THREE entries in the general ledger?**

General ledger

Account name	Amount £	Debit ✓	Credit ✓
▼			
▼			
▼			

Picklist:

Abunda Bags
Bank
Discounts allowed
Discounts received
Purchases
Purchases ledger control
Sales
Sales ledger control
VAT

Task 5

Sumberton Ltd maintains a petty cash-book as a book of prime entry and part of the double entry bookkeeping system. This is a summary of petty cash transactions in a week.

Stamps bought for £12.60, VAT not applicable.
Staplers bought for £18.90, including VAT.

(a) **Enter the above transactions into the partially completed petty cash-book below.**

(b) **Total the petty cash-book and show the balance carried down.**

Petty cash-book

Details	Amount £	Details	Amount £	VAT £	Postage £	Stationery £
Balance b/f	175.00	Printer cartridges	17.40	2.90		14.50
Total		Totals				

Picklist:

Balance b/f
Balance c/d
Postage
Stamps
Staplers
Stationery
VAT

(c) **What will be the THREE accounts in the general ledger which will record the above transactions?**

General ledger accounts	
Stamps	
Stationery	
Petty cash-book	
Petty cash control	
Postage	
Staplers	
VAT	

(d) **Complete the following statement by choosing ONE word.**

In order to top up the petty cash to the imprest amount, the petty cashier needs to prepare a

Remittance advice note	
Cheque requisition form	
Petty cash claim	
Customer statement	

At the start of the next week cash was withdrawn from the bank to restore the imprest level of £175.

(e) **What is the amount of cash that would have been withdrawn from the bank to restore the imprest level?**

£ [   ]

These are the notes and coins that are now in the petty cash box.

Notes and coins
3 × £20 notes
2 x £10 notes
3 × £5 notes
14 × £1 coins
3 × 50p coins
3 × 20p coins

(f) **Does the amount of cash in the petty cash box reconcile with the balance in the petty cash-book?**

Yes, the amount of cash in the petty cash box reconciles with the balance in the petty cash-book	
No, there is not enough cash in the petty cash box	
No, there is too much cash in the petty cash box	

Task 6

Below is a list of balances to be transferred to the trial balance as at 30 November.

Place the figures in the debit or credit column, as appropriate, and total each column. Do not enter figures with decimal places in this task and do not enter a zero in the empty column.

Account name	Amount £	Debit £	Credit £
Maintenance expenses	6,082		
Cash at bank	22,241		
Capital	24,000		
Heat and light	7,893		
Discounts allowed	2,409		
Discounts received	7,056		
Motor expenses	7,435		
Machinery	36,000		
Computer equipment	8,018		
Sundry expenses	14,167		
Legal expenses	1,195		
Office expenses	1,221		
Petty cash	200		
Purchases	214,229		
Purchases ledger control	17,851		
Rent and rates	6,976		
Sales	421,956		
Sales ledger control	28,540		
Sales returns	7,252		
Inventory	38,414		
Bank interest received	1,253		
Travel	1,096		
VAT (owing to HM Revenue & Customs)	15,892		
Salaries	84,640		
Totals			

Task 7

A supply of suitcases has been delivered to Sumberton Ltd by Casaubon's. The purchase order sent from Sumberton Ltd, and the invoice from Casaubon's, are shown below.

Sumberton Ltd
Sumberton House, 10 Main Road
Sawlow
SA7 5LD

Purchase Order No. 7683247

To: Casaubon's

Date: 17 December 20XX

Please supply 15 small wheeled cabin cases, product code WCC625
Purchase price: £23 each, plus VAT
Discount: less 15% trade discount, as agreed.

Casaubon's
80 Eliot Street, Sawlow SA9 4AC
VAT Registration No. 983 3933 83

Invoice No. 782736

Sumberton Ltd
Sumberton House, 10 Main Road
Sawlow
SA7 5LD

22 December 20XX

15 small wheeled cabin cases product code WCC625 @ £25 each	£375.00
Less trade discount at 5%	£18.75
Net amount	£356.25
VAT @ 20%	£71.25
Total	£427.50

Terms: 30 days net

(a) **Check the invoice against the purchase order and answer the following questions.**

	Yes ✓	No ✓
Has the correct purchase price of the cabin cases been charged?		
Has the correct discount been applied?		
What would be the VAT amount charged if the invoice was correct?	£	
What would be the total amount charged if the invoice was correct?	£	

Shown below is a statement of account received from a credit supplier, and the supplier's account as shown in the purchases ledger of Sumberton Ltd.

Trinder and Papp
54 Vallais Road
Gosfirth
GO9 5VV

To: Sumberton Ltd
Sumberton House
10 Main Road
Sawlow
SA7 5LD

STATEMENT OF ACCOUNT

Date 20XX	Number	Details	Amount £	Balance £
20 October	10923	Invoice	2,109	2,109
4 November		Payment	−2,099	10
8 November	11004	Invoice	3,188	3,198
10 November	C536	Credit note	−156	3,042
26 November	11342	Invoice	2,185	5,227
28 November	11378	Invoice	1,244	6,471
30 November	C579	Credit note	−320	6,151

Trinder and Papp

Date 20XX	Details	Amount £	Date 20XX	Details	Amount £
4 Nov	Bank – BACS	2,099	20 Oct	Purchases	2,109
4 Nov	Discount	10	8 Nov	Purchases	3,188
10 Nov	Purchases returns	156	26 Nov	Purchases	2,185
			28 Nov	Purchases	1,244

(b) **Which item is missing from the statement of account from Trinder and Papp?**

	▼

Picklist:

Credit note C536
Credit note C579
Discount of £10
Invoice 10923
Invoice 11004
Invoice 11342
Invoice 11378
Payment for £2,099

(c) **Which item is missing from the supplier account in Sumberton Ltd's purchases ledger?**

	▼

Picklist:

Credit note C536
Credit note C579
Discount of £10
Invoice 10923
Invoice 11004
Invoice 11342
Invoice 11378
Payment for £2,099

(d) **Assuming any differences between the statement of account from Trinder and Papp and the supplier account in Sumberton Ltd's purchases ledger are simply due to omission errors, what is the amount owing to Trinder and Papp?**

£ _____

(e) **Which of the following statements is True?**

	✓
A credit note adds to the amount owed to the supplier	
A remittance advice note adds to the amount owed to the supplier	
A goods received note adds to the amount owed to the supplier	
An invoice adds to the amount owed to the supplier	

Task 8

On 21 December Sumberton Ltd delivered the following goods to a credit customer, Gringles Co.

Sumberton Ltd
Sumberton House
10 Main Road
Sawlow
SA7 5LD

Delivery note No. 6734527
21 December 20XX

Gringles Co   Customer account code: SL637
Unit 18 Radley Estate
Sawlow
SA7 7VB

80 leather shoulder bags, product code L736B.

The list price of the goods was £100 per box of five bags plus VAT. Gringles Co is to be given a 15% bulk discount and a 4% discount if the invoice is paid within 10 days.

(a) **Complete the invoice below.**

Sumberton Ltd
Sumberton House,
10 Main Road
Sawlow
SA7 5LD

VAT Registration No. 536 3723 77

Gringles Co   Customer account code: SL637
Unit 18 Radley Estate
Sawlow
SA7 7VB

                                                    Date: 22 December 20XX
Invoice No: 12901
Delivery note number: 6734527

Quantity of goods	Product code	Total list price £	Net amount after bulk discount £	VAT £	Gross £

Sumberton Ltd offers some established customers a discount of 4% whatever the size of their order and irrespective of when they pay.

(b) **What is the name of this type of discount?**

Picklist:

Bulk discount
Settlement discount
Trade discount

The account shown below is in the sales ledger of Sumberton Ltd. A remittance advice for an automated payment of £2,807 has now been received from this customer.

Meering Ltd

Date 20XX	Details	Amount £	Date 20XX	Details	Amount £
6 October	Sales invoice 12624	1,756	10 October	Sales returns credit note 501	78
11 November	Sales invoice 12711	2,918	17 November	Sales returns credit note 555	111
7 December	Sales invoice 12813	2,384	30 November	Bank	1,678

(c) **Which outstanding item has not been included in the payment of £2,807?**

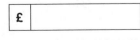

Picklist:

Sales invoice 12624   Sales invoice 12813
Sales invoice 12711   Bank
Sales returns credit note 501   Sales returns credit note 555

An invoice is being prepared to be sent to Meering Ltd for £2,000 plus VAT of £384. A settlement discount of 4% will be offered for payment within 10 days.

(d) **What is the amount Sumberton Ltd should receive if payment is made within 10 days?**

£

(e) **What is the amount Sumberton Ltd should receive if payment is NOT made within 10 days?**

£

Task 9

The following two accounts are in the general ledger at the close of day on 30 November.

(a) **Insert the balance carried down together with date and details.**
(b) **Insert the totals.**
(c) **Insert the balance brought down together with date and details.**

Purchases

Date 20XX	Details	Amount £	Date 20XX	Details	Amount £
01 Nov	Balance b/d	140,389		▼	
15 Nov	Purchases ledger control	14,388		▼	
30 Nov	Purchases ledger control	52,389		▼	
		▼		▼	
	Total			Total	
		▼		▼	

Picklist:

Balance b/d
Balance c/d
Bank
Purchases
Purchases ledger control
Sales ledger control

Bank interest received

Date 20XX	Details	Amount £	Date 20XX	Details	Amount £
	▼		01 Nov	Balance b/d	32
	▼		15 Nov	Bank	14
	▼		30 Nov	Bank	22
	▼			▼	
	Total			Total	
	▼			▼	

Picklist:

Balance b/d
Balance c/d
Bank
Bank interest received
Purchases ledger control
Sales ledger control

The following is a summary of transactions with Diamond Bags, a new credit customer.

£1,902 re invoice 12905 of 10 December
£219 re credit note 701 of 12 December
£733 re invoice 12916 of 30 December
Cheque for £1,668 received 31 December
Settlement discount £15 taken 31 December

(d) **Complete the statement of account below.**

Sumberton Ltd
Sumberton House
10 Main Road
Sawlow
SA7 5LD

To: Diamond Bags   Date: 31 December 20XX

Date 20XX	Details	Transaction amount £	Outstanding amount £
10 December	Invoice 12905		
12 December	Credit note 701		
30 December	Invoice 12916		
31 December	Cheque		
31 December	Discount taken		

Task 10

It is important to understand the difference between capital expenditure, revenue expenditure, capital income and revenue income.

(a) **Select one option in each instance below to show whether the item will be capital expenditure, revenue expenditure, capital income or revenue income.**

Item	Capital expenditure ✓	Revenue expenditure ✓	Capital income ✓	Revenue income ✓
Payment in advance for 3 months of phone line rental				
Proceeds from sale of machinery				
Sale of suitcases for cash				
Receipt of payment from trade receivable for bags				
Purchase of a shop building				
Petty cash payment for stationery				

(b) **Show whether the following statements are True or False.**

	True ✓	False ✓
The book of original entry for discounts allowed is the petty cash book		
Input tax is the VAT suffered on purchases		
A goods received note is a primary document for recording in the accounting records		

(c) **For each of the items below, identify an example from the picklist provided.**

Item	Example
Asset	▼
Liability	▼
Capital transaction	▼

Picklist:

Drawings
Trade receivables
Bank overdraft

BPP PRACTICE ASSESSMENT 4
PROCESSING BOOKKEEPING
TRANSACTIONS

ANSWERS

Processing Bookkeeping Transactions BPP practice assessment 4

Task 1

(a) – (b)

Sales returns day book

Date 20XX	Details	Credit note number	Total £	VAT @ 20% £	Net £	Bags returns £	Suitcases returns £
30 Nov	Shrier Goods	562	624	104	520	520	
30 Nov	Gringles Co	563	408	68	340		340
30 Nov	Lester plc	564	1,068	178	890	890	
	Totals		2,100	350	1,750	1,410	340

(c)

Supplier code	PL244
General ledger code	GL001

(d) The correct answer is: Product code

Task 2

(a)

Sales ledger

Account name	Amount £	Debit ✓	Credit ✓
Gringles Co	300	✓	
Lester plc	1,308	✓	
Shrier Goods	2,676	✓	
Abunda Bags	1,992	✓	

(b)

General ledger

Account name	Amount £	Debit ✓	Credit ✓
Sales ledger control	6,276	✓	
Sales	5,230		✓
VAT	1,046		✓

(c)

Purchases ledger

Account name	Amount £	Debit ✓	Credit ✓
Frankie's Leatherware	12,348		✓
Casaubon's	3,924		✓

(d)

General ledger

Account name	Amount £	Debit ✓	Credit ✓
Purchases ledger control	16,272		✓
Purchases	13,560	✓	
VAT	2,712	✓	

Task 3

(a)

Cash book – debit side

Details	Discounts £	Cash £	Bank £	VAT £	Trade receivables £	Cash sales £
Balance b/f		159	844			
Humber & Co		582		97		485
Ridgely Ltd	72		2,150		2,150	
Watts Partners	25		978		978	
Total	97	741	3,972	97	3,128	485

(b) The correct answer is: £ 180 (£741 – £561)

(c) The correct answer is: £ –113 (£3,972 – £4,085)

Task 4

(a)

Purchases ledger

Account name	Amount £	Debit ✓	Credit ✓
Casaubon's	2,445	✓	

(b)

General ledger

Account name	Amount £	Debit ✓	Credit ✓
Purchases ledger control	2,445	✓	
Purchases	510	✓	
VAT	102	✓	

(c)

General ledger

Account name	Amount £	Debit ✓	Credit ✓
Sales ledger control	3,984		✓
Sales ledger control	56		✓
Discounts allowed	56	✓	

Task 5

(a) – (b)

Petty cash-book

Details	Amount £	Details	Amount £	VAT £	Postage £	Stationery £
Balance b/f	175.00	Printer cartridges	17.40	2.90		14.50
		Stamps	12.60		12.60	
		Staplers	18.90	3.15		15.75
		Balance c/d	126.10			
Total	175.00	Totals	175.00	6.05	12.60	30.25

Working: £18.90 × 20/120 = £3.15 VAT

(c)

General ledger accounts	
Stamps	
Stationery	✓
Petty cash-book	
Petty cash control	
Postage	✓
Staplers	
VAT	✓

(d)

Remittance advice note	
Cheque requisition form	✓
Petty cash claim	
Customer statement	

(e) The correct answer is: £48.90 (£17.40 + £12.60 + £18.90)

(f) The correct answer is: No, there is not enough cash in the petty cash box

Task 6

Account name	Amount £	Debit £	Credit £
Maintenance expenses	6,082	6,082	
Cash at bank	22,241	22,241	
Capital	24,000		24,000
Heat and light	7,893	7,893	
Discounts allowed	2,409	2,409	
Discounts received	7,056		7,056
Motor expenses	7,435	7,435	
Machinery	36,000	36,000	
Computer equipment	8,018	8,018	
Sundry expenses	14,167	14,167	
Legal expenses	1,195	1,195	
Office expenses	1,221	1,221	
Petty cash	200	200	
Purchases	214,229	214,229	
Purchases ledger control	17,851		17,851
Rent and rates	6,976	6,976	
Sales	421,956		421,956
Sales ledger control	28,540	28,540	
Sales returns	7,252	7,252	
Inventory	38,414	38,414	
Bank interest received	1,253		1,253
Travel	1,096	1,096	
VAT (owing to HM Revenue & Customs)	15,892		15,892
Salaries	84,640	84,640	
Totals		488,008	488,008

Task 7

(a)

VAT: (15 × 23) × 0.85 × 0.2 = 58.65

Total: (15 × 23 × 0.85) + 58.65 = 351.90

	Yes ✓	No ✓
Has the correct purchase price of the cabin cases been charged?		✓
Has the correct discount been applied?		✓
What would be the VAT amount charged if the invoice was correct?	£	58.65
What would be the total amount charged if the invoice was correct?	£	351.90

(b) The correct answer is: discount of £10

(c) The correct answer is: credit note C579

(d) The correct answer is: £6,141

Working

(6,151 – 10)

(e) The correct answer is: An invoice adds to the amount owed to the supplier

Task 8

(a)

Sumberton Ltd
Sumberton House,
10 Main Road
Sawlow
SA7 5LD

VAT Registration No. 536 3723 77

Gringles Co	Customer account code: SL637
Unit 18 Radley Estate	
Sawlow	
SA7 7VB	

Date: 22 December 20XX

Invoice No: 12901
Delivery note number: 6734527

Quantity of goods	Product code	Total list price £	Net amount after bulk discount £	VAT £	Gross £
80	L736B	1,600.00	1,360.00	261.12	1,621.12

(b) The correct answer is: trade discount

(c) The correct answer is: Sales invoice 12813

(d) The correct answer is: £2,304 ((2,000 × 96/100) + 384)

(e) The correct answer is: £2,384 (2,000 + 384)

Task 9

(a) – (c)

Purchases

Date 20XX	Details	Amount £	Date 20XX	Details	Amount £
01 Nov	Balance b/d	140,389			
15 Nov	Purchases ledger control	14,388			
30 Nov	Purchases ledger control	52,389			
			30 Nov	Balance c/d	207,166
	Total	207,166		Total	207,166
1 Dec	Balance b/d	207,166			

Bank interest received

Date 20XX	Details	Amount £	Date 20XX	Details	Amount £
			01 Nov	Balance b/d	32
			15 Nov	Bank	14
			30 Nov	Bank	22
30 Nov	Balance c/d	68			
	Total	68		Total	68
			1 Dec	Balance b/d	68

(d)

Sumberton Ltd
Sumberton House
10 Main Road
Sawlow
SA7 5LD

To: Diamond Bags
Date: 31 December 20XX

Date 20XX	Details	Transaction amount £	Outstanding amount £
10 December	Invoice 12905	1,902	1,902
12 December	Credit note 701	219	1,683
30 December	Invoice 12916	733	2,416
31 December	Cheque	1,668	748
31 December	Discount taken	15	733

Task 10

(a)

Item	Capital expenditure ✓	Revenue expenditure ✓	Capital income ✓	Revenue income ✓
Payment in advance for 3 months of phone line rental		✓		
Proceeds from sale of machinery			✓	
Sale of suitcases for cash				✓
Receipt of payment from trade receivable for bags				✓
Purchase of a shop building	✓			
Petty cash payment for stationery		✓		

(b)

	True ✓	False ✓
The book of original entry for discounts allowed is the petty cash book		✓
Input tax is the VAT suffered on purchases	✓	
A goods received note is a primary document for recording in the accounting records		✓

(c)

Item	Example
Asset	Trade receivables
Liability	Bank overdraft
Capital transaction	Drawings